THE BUBBLE THAT
BROKE THE BANK

Survival Strategies for Navigating the Real

Estate Crash, 2008-2026

BY

CHARLES S HERRERA

Grand Empire Books (GEP, LLC)

Dedication

This dedication is a tribute to my wife, Gloria. You are the Hawaiian rainbow that has filled my heart with vibrant colors and brought light to every corner of my life. Your unwavering love and support have been the anchor that has kept me grounded through the highs and lows of my journey as a writer. From the moment that we met, I knew that our bond was something special, a rare and precious gift that I would cherish forever.

Acknowledgement

I want to express my gratitude to the following individuals and works that have had a significant impact on my journey as a writer: Nick Gerli and the Real Estate Youtubers, Howard Marks, Adam Tooze, Crashed, Cathie Wood of Ark Invest, Hyun Song Shin, the AI Revolution in Real Estate, Dr. Kai Fu Lee ground breaking research in AI, Arizona State University, and Paradise Valley College.

In closing, I want to express my deepest gratitude to everyone who helped me along the way, including those whose names I have not mentioned here. Your support, guidance, and inspiration have been instrumental in shaping the person I am today, and I am honored to be to work with you all.

Preface

The once solid banking institutions were like fully blown ballons solid to the sight but easily destroyed with a single pinprick.

Robert Soble, Panic on Wall Street

Enter the world of financial enchantment and disillusionment through the pages of Garet Garett's A Bubble That Broke the World. Transport yourself back to the 1920s, when the masses were consumed by the feverish desire for limitless riches and unending debt. Garett's fascinating work was devoured by many, as it exposed the delusions that led to the infamous financial bubble of this era.

Fast forward to the present day, and we find ourselves grappling with a similar crisis as the Silicon Valley Bank, once the 16th largest bank, lost over 48 billion dollars of depositor funds.

This bizarre case is just the tip of the iceberg, as economic Nobel Prize winner Dr. Douglas Diamond astutely points out. He argues that modern banking's Achilles heel lies in the relentless pursuit of profits, which has led to a looming economic banking disaster.

Drawing on the insights of Adam Tooze's acclaimed work Crashed, we explore the catastrophic consequences of the subprime real estate meltdown, devastating events that threatened to destabilize the entire global financial system.

Hyun Song Shin's interlocking matrix of the transatlantic banking balance sheet is a complex web of financial interdependence that connects the banks of Europe and the United States. At the heart of this interlocking matrix lies the concept of "Pro-Cyclicality." This refers to the tendency of financial institutions to amplify and propagate economic cycles rather than dampen them.

Hyun Song Shin's research study on the collapse of Northern Rock, the 5th largest bank in the U.K., makes a shocking discovery. He found that "The Northern Rock Bank run was not enacted by individuals, but sophisticated institutional investors." The media showed people in line waiting for their money, but the real withdrawals were coming from sophisticated institutional investors.

In other words, when times are good, banks tend to take on more risk and leverage, which can exacerbate economic booms. And when times are bad, banks tend to deleverage and reduce their risk exposure, which can deepen and prolong economic downturns. The balance sheets of these banks are tightly interconnected, with assets and liabilities spread across borders, making the financial system highly vulnerable to shocks and disturbances.

In their book <u>AI 2041</u>, Dr. Kai Fu Lee and Chen Quifan outline the numerous advantages of using AI as a Superforecasting tool. With AI's ability to analyze large amounts of data, identify patterns and trends, and make accurate predictions based on historical data., real estate investors and developers can make more informed decisions about where and when to invest their resources. AI can also help to minimize risk and maximize returns by identifying potential opportunities and potential pitfalls. By harnessing the power of AI, the real estate industry can become more efficient, sustainable, and profitable, creating a better future for all involved.

When it comes to predicting the future, Artificial Intelligence has a lot of advantages over human beings, and it's not hard to see why. Imagine a machine that can process vast amounts of data at lightning speed, never gets tired, never makes mistakes due to biases or emotions, and learns from its mistakes to become even better at predicting outcomes. That's the power of AI, and it's a force to be reckoned with in the world of forecasting and prediction.

The upcoming crash in 2026, the 18.6 Real Estate Cycle, will have far-reaching implications for the American banking system, from loan defaults to investor confidence, tighter lending standards, to increase foreclosures. The Bubble That Broke the Bank aims to equip readers with the tools to navigate this treacherous terrain, akin to Odysseus resisting the hypnotic Siren calls that once led to ships crashing against the rocks.

Like the mythical hero, we, too, can learn from

the bitter lessons of the past to seek out the elusive golden fleece of investment. So, come aboard this journey of financial education and enlightenment, and brace yourself for the challenges that lie ahead.

Contents

About the Author

Charles S. Herrera, Ph.D., is a historian, entrepreneur, educator, and award-winning professor at Paradise Valley College. He has been recognized as Professor of the Year for his dedication to teaching and research. Dr. Herrera has been involved in research on the economic, demographic, and housing markets for more than 10 years. Dr. Herrera has developed the Artificial Intelligence Nexus AI Model. Dr. Herrera's Nexus AI Model integrates predictive analytics with the Real Estate Cycle.

He is currently working on a new historical novel that explores the rich ancient history of Hawaii. His deep knowledge of the subject and his ability to weave engaging narratives makes him the perfect person to bring this fascinating story to life.

Page Blank Intentionally

Chapter 1

The Housing Crisis Chronicles: 2008 AD

"That was the problem with money: What people did with it had consequences, but they were so remote from the original action that the mind never connected the one with the other."

-Michael Lewis, The Big Short: Inside the Doomsday Machine

The rapid expansion of the subprime mortgage market, which started in 1999, was a major factor in laying the groundwork for the chaos that would erupt in the housing market and stock market in 2008. These events occurred just nine years later, in 2008.

This time period was one of the most catastrophic in the history of the financial markets in the United States. Those who were there and experienced the upheaval firsthand are highly unlikely to forget it.

In October 1999, the subprime was in the early phases of a growing disaster. Adriana Rodriguez and her husband bought into the lower middle-class dream of owning their own home. She worked as an administrative technician in a dental office, and her husband had a blue-collar job as a forklift operator.

She and her husband applied for an adjustable-rate mortgage that would allow them to do a cash-out refinance. She would have enough money to do home improvement. She did not realize these loans came with high-interest rates and higher mortgage payments. She believed the loan officer that the rate would go down in the future.

In the early 2000s, Nicholas Cage was living the high life, enjoying the fruits of his labor as a successful actor. With his fame and fortune, Cage built an impressive real estate empire, spanning across the country and even across the Atlantic Ocean.

He owned a total of 15 residences, including homes in California, Nevada, and New Orleans, and even castles in Germany and England. Each property was more lavish than the last, featuring amenities like a vineyard, a moat, and stunning views of the Pacific Ocean.

However, Cage's real estate empire was not immune to the financial crisis that struck the United States in 2007. "I was over-invested in real estate," he said. "The real estate market crashed, and I couldn't get out in Time."

He had overextended himself, taking out numerous mortgages on his properties, and when the housing market crashed, he was unable to keep up with payments.

As a result, Cage was forced to part ways with his stunning 25-million-dollar waterfront home in Newport Beach, California, a 24,000-square-foot mansion in Las Vegas that he reportedly bought for 8.5 million dollars, and even his beloved castles in Europe. He was also faced with legal and financial issues, including a lawsuit against his former business manager and over 6 million dollars in unpaid taxes owed to the IRS.

The 2008 crash happened, and the Rodriguez's could not make the payments. Her husband lost his job, and the mortgage payments skyrocketed. She eventually had to sell her house. Her husband divorced her, and she ended up making hopeless payments. "I just don't even want to go there, she shouts. "I have friends who have recovered from it and have purchased homes. But I don't know where to start. It's just hard. You don't ever want to go through that again."

The 2008 real estate market crash was a major financial crisis that occurred in the United States and had ripple effects throughout the world. The crisis was caused by a combination of factors, including a housing bubble, a proliferation of subprime mortgages, and the widespread use of complex financial instruments that were difficult to understand and value.

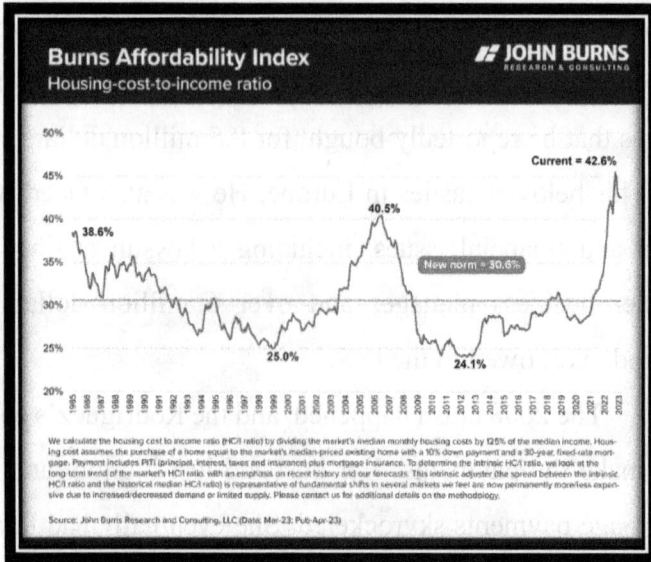

Beginning in the early 2000s, the U.S. housing market experienced a boom characterized by swiftly rising home prices and an increase in new construction. Countless people took advantage of low-interest rates to purchase unaffordable homes, and lenders were all too willing to provide them with hazardous loans, frequently without verifying their income or creditworthiness.

The unprecedented development of the subprime mortgage market, which started in 1999 and continued until 2008, is considered to be the root cause of the collapses that occurred in the stock market and the housing market in 2008. We will explore this further in this chapter.

INSIDE THE DOOM'S DAY MACHINE

As the number of subprime mortgages increased, so did the number of defaults, leading to a decline in the value of mortgage-backed securities (MBS) that were based on these loans. This caused panic among investors, who began selling off their holdings, leading to a downward spiral in the value of MBS and other complex financial instruments.

Subprime mortgages are given to debtors with less-than-perfect credit and insufficient savings. In 1999, the U.S. government-sponsored mortgage lender Federal National Mortgage Association (commonly known as Fannie Mae) launched a concerted effort to make home loans more accessible to borrowers with lower credit and savings than conventional lenders required.

The Federal National Mortgage Association is a government-backed organization. It provides liquidity for home purchases, the financing of multifamily rental housing, and the refinancing of existing mortgages. The business is divided into the following segments: Single- and multifamily dwellings. The Single-Family segment provides mortgage market liquidity and increases the availability and affordability of housing for single-family households.

The Multifamily segment contains mortgage and multifamily mortgage loan guarantee fees. Federal National

Mortgage Association was established in 1938 and had its headquarters in Washington, District of Columbia.

The intention was to assist everyone in achieving the American ideal of homeownership. Since these borrowers were deemed high-risk, their mortgages had unconventional provisions, such as higher interest rates and variable payments, to reflect this risk. The explosion of the subprime market was met with euphoria by many, but alarm bells were rung by those who saw the signs of impending economic disaster.

Since the mortgage industry as a whole is reliant on rising property values, Elliott Wave International founder Robert R. Prechter Jr. has long warned that the mortgage market was out of control and posed a threat to the U.S. economy.

By 2002, Fannie Mae and Freddie Mac, another government-sponsored mortgage provider, had provided over three trillion dollars in mortgage loans. When mortgage notes are settled in full, Fannie Mae and Freddie Mac repurchase them from the original lenders. As a result, these two businesses saw a dramatic drop in income due to rising mortgage default rates.

The interest-only ARM and the payment option ARM were among the riskiest mortgages available to subprime debtors. Both debts had variable interest rates (ARMS). In comparison to what would be required under a fixed-rate mortgage, the borrower can start making payments on these kinds of loans at much lower rates.

These adjustable rate mortgages (ARMs) reset after a set length of time, typically two to three years, at typically higher rates. The borrower's obligations could increase by a significant amount, sometimes every month, before stabilizing.

These mortgages were extremely low risk during the period of time (1999-2005) when the market was trending upward (and the housing bubble was expanding). If the value of the borrower's house has increased since the purchase date, then even if the monthly mortgage payment is small, the borrower may eventually have positive equity. After their mortgage rates were adjusted, they could sell the houses for a profit if they were unable to afford the new, higher payments.

Others, however, warned that a downturn in the housing market would spell catastrophe for homeowners who took out these "creative mortgages," as they would be stuck in a negative equity position and unable to sell.

A credit derivative, also known as a credit default swap, was a prominent investment vehicle during this period

(CDS). CDSs were created as an insurance-like means of safeguarding against a company's creditworthiness. The CDS market, however, was unregulated, unlike the insurance market.

This meant that there was no requirement for CDS contract issuers to maintain sufficient reserves to pay out in a worst-case scenario (such as an economic downturn). When American International Group (AIG), one of the nation's leading financial institutions, was unable to meet claims and announced massive losses in its portfolio of underwritten CDS contracts in early 2008, it signaled a potential disaster.

Bear Stearns collapsed in March 2007 after incurring massive losses from underwriting numerous investment vehicles associated with the subprime housing market. It became clear that the market was in danger and that the subprime mortgage crisis was imminent. As home prices fell, inventive variations of subprime mortgages reset to higher payments, resulting in a high default rate among homeowners.

It was no longer possible for homeowners to simply flip their homes in order to avoid paying the new, higher mortgage payments because they were "upside down," owing more on their loans than their properties were currently worth. Instead, they lost their residences through foreclosure and frequently filed for bankruptcy. The subprime mortgage crisis was affecting homeowners and the real estate market.

Despite this evident chaos, the financial markets continued to rise throughout October 2007, with the Dow Jones Industrial Average (DJIA) closing at 14,164 on October 9, 2007.

In December 2007, the United States fell into a recession as a result of the turmoil. By the beginning of July 2008, the Dow Jones Industrial Average would fall below 11,000 for the first time in more than two years.

That would not mark the conclusion of the decline.

The government declared the takeover of Fannie Mae and Freddie Mac on September 6, 2008, after the financial markets had fallen by nearly 20% from their October 2007 highs. It was necessary to take this action due to losses sustained from exposure to the subprime mortgage market's collapse.

The crisis reached a peak in September 2008, when the investment bank Lehman Brothers filed for bankruptcy, triggering a wider financial panic that threatened to bring down the entire financial system. The U.S. government responded with a series of emergency measures, including a massive bailout of the financial sector and the creation of new regulations designed to prevent a similar crisis from happening in the future.

The collapse of Lehman caused the Reserve Primary Fund's net asset value to decline below 1 dollar per share on September 16, 2008. Buyers were told that they would only receive 97 cents on every dollar they put in. The holding of commercial paper that was issued by Lehman was the cause of this decline, which was only the second time in the history of money market funds that the share value "broke the buck."

The money market fund industry descended into panic, resulting in enormous redemption requests. Bank of America (BAC) announced the acquisition of Merrill Lynch, the nation's largest brokerage firm, on the same day. In addition, American International Group's credit rating was lowered as a direct result of the credit derivative arrangements that were underwritten by the company in the previous paragraph.

On September 18, 2008, rumors of a government rescue began, causing the Dow to increase by 410 points.

The following day, Treasury Secretary Henry Paulson proposed an up to 1 trillion dollar Troubled Asset Relief Program (TARP) to purchase toxic debt and prevent a complete financial catastrophe.

To stabilize the markets, the Securities and Exchange Commission (SEC) instituted a temporary prohibition on short-selling financial company stocks on this date.

The news caused a spike in trading activity across global markets, and investors drove the Dow Jones Industrial Average up 456 points to an intraday high of 11,483 before sending it down 361 points to end the day at 11,388.

These peaks would prove to be historically significant as the financial markets were about to experience three weeks of complete chaos.

Do you ever wonder what the top investors know that the rest of us don't? Well, back in 2008, it was all about understanding the real estate and credit cycle. Those who cracked the code knew exactly how to position themselves to make a killing.

REAL ESTATE CYCLE POSITIONING

One such savvy investor was Howard Marks," co-founder of Oaktree Capital Management. He used his market cycle knowledge to invest a jaw-dropping 10 billion dollars in just fifteen weeks. That's some serious cash flow!

Now, you might be thinking, "Well, that's all well and good for the bigwigs on Wall Street," but what about us regular folks/" Don't worry, my friend. The truth is, anyone can use this forecasting skill to their advantage. By understanding the market cycles, you, too, can position yourself for success and potentially create your own instant future.

So, let me ask you this: are you ready to learn the secrets of the market cycle and take control of your financial future? With a little know-how and some strategic positioning, you could be well on your way to financial freedom.

What was the secret formula for 2008? The formula was within the real estate cycle. The individuals who understood how to use cycle positioning created an instant fortune. Howard Marks, the co-founder of Oaktree Capital Management, used cycle positioning to invest 10 billion dollars in fifteen weeks.

He created a massive return on investment for his investors. The Marks Matrix was a great discovery by harvesting a combination of the credit cycle combined with the real estate cycle. He had calculated that using Altman's Z scores would lead him to financial distress companies.

Howard Marks was able to create a timetable and used the cycle positioning to plan his entry and exit to the credit-distressed companies. Ironically, Oaktree Capital Management has set up a new fund to harvest the coming real estate crash. This is the power of cycle positioning!

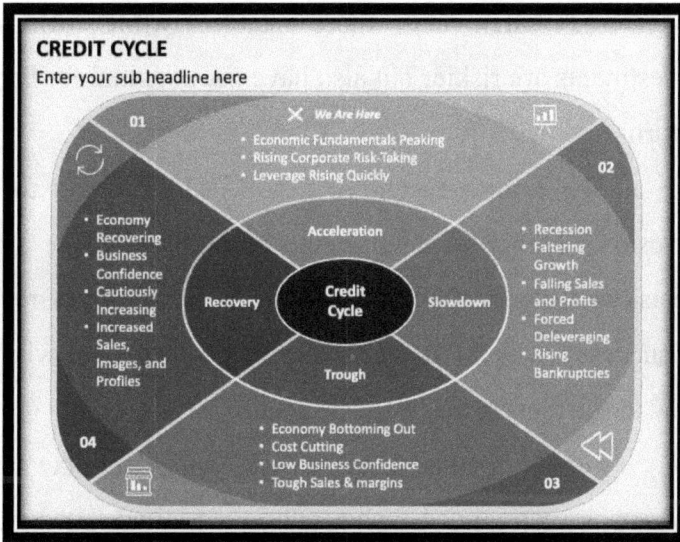

The first factor is the cycle position, which refers to where the real estate market is in its 18.6-Year cycle. This could be a boom, a bust, or somewhere in between. Understanding where the market is in the 18.6-Year cycle can help investors make more informed decisions about when to buy or sell properties.

The second factor is the asset, which refers to the type of real estate being invested in. This could be residential, commercial, industrial, or other types of properties. Each type of asset has its own unique characteristics and risks, so investors need to consider these factors when making investment decisions.

The third factor is whether the investment is defensive or offensive. Defensive investments are typically considered safer and more stable, while offensive investments are riskier but also have the potential for higher returns.

The Fourth factor is a skill, which refers to the investor's ability to analyze the market and make smart decisions. Experienced investors with a strong track record of success are likely to have better results than those who are new to the market.

Finally, the last factor is luck, which can play a role in any investment. Unexpected events such as natural disasters, economic downturns, or other factors can impact the success of an invest, even if the investor has done everything right.

Why should the average consumer or investor use cycle positioning? This book is designed to be a practical guide for those individuals who want to avoid the 2008 tragedy. It will explain how the understanding real estate cycle works and how to plan entry and exit positions. It gives a series of money-making strategies and investment strategies for individuals.

What are the key factors that create real estate wealth?

*The 18.6-year real estate cycle suggests that real estate prices follow a predictable pattern, which can provide investors with a framework for making informed investment decisions.

*During the expansion phase of the real estate cycle, real estate prices tend to rise steadily, which can lead to significant wealth creation for investors who own property.

*During the contraction phase of the real estate cycle, real estate prices may decline, but this presents opportunities for savvy investors and homeowners to purchase undervalued properties that can provide a foundation for future wealth creation.

*By understanding and tracking the 18.6-year real estate cycle, investors can make more informed decisions about when to buy, hold, or sell real estate assets, which can help to maximize returns and minimize risks.

*Real estate investing can provide multiple streams of income, including rental income, capital gains, and tax benefits, which can all contribute to long-term wealth.

Moreover, it answers the question of when I should buy or sell my real estate properties. What is more important interest rates or purchase price? How long will the downturn last? Why should I buy a new home at the bottom of the real estate cycle? When will the recovery happen in the United States? What are the specific timeframes that I can use for my investments?

The 2008 real estate market crash had far-reaching consequences, including a global recession, millions of foreclosures, and a loss of confidence in the financial system. It also led to significant changes in the way that banks and other financial institutions operate, with a greater emphasis on transparency and risk management.

Chapter Two

The End of Easy Money

"A thought crossed his mind: How do you make poor people feel wealthy when wages are stagnant? You give them cheap loans."

-Michael Lewis, The Big Short: Inside the Doomsday Machine

Interest rates are the primary instrument used by the Federal Reserve and the U.S. central bank to manage inflation. Therefore, inflation and interest rates tend to move in the same direction.

The relationship between inflation and interest rates is generally inverse, meaning that as inflation increases, interest rates tend to go up, and as inflation decreases, interest rates tend to go down.

When inflation is high, central banks may raise interest rates to reduce the money supply, thereby increasing the cost of borrowing and decreasing consumer demand. This can help to reduce inflation by reducing the quantity of money available for spending and slowing economic growth.

Conversely, when inflation is low, central banks may lower interest rates to encourage borrowing and stimulate economic activity. This can increase demand for goods and services and lead to higher inflation over time.

Increases in the federal funds rate, the Fed's benchmark rate, in response to rising inflationary pressures, have the impact of raising the total amount of risk-free reserves in the financial system, thereby reducing the amount of money available for investment in riskier assets.

In contrast, when a central bank lowers its goal interest rate, more money is made available to buy risky assets.

THE HOUSE MONEY EFFECT

Now, why are rising interest rates worrisome? Rising interest rates reduce spending by households and businesses because they make borrowing more expensive, particularly for large, frequently financed purchases like homes and office machinery. The wealth impact on individuals is reversed, and banks become more conservative as a result of rising interest rates.

Last but not least, a hike in interest rates is an indication that the Fed is likely to keep pushing for monetary tightening, which should have the effect of reducing inflation expectations even further.

The greatest expense of inflation is the erosion of real income that occurs as a result of rising prices that affect different groups of people in various ways.

Over time, both the recipients and the payers of fixed interest rates may see their buying power distorted due to inflation.

We will study Mike's case as an example. Mike is a pensioner and receives a fixed 5 percent yearly increase to his pension. If inflation exceeds 5 percent, a pensioner's purchasing power declines. On the other hand, a borrower with a 5-percent fixed-rate mortgage would benefit from 5-percent inflation because the real interest rate (nominal rate minus inflation rate) would be zero.

Paying off this debt would be even easier if inflation was higher, as long as the borrower's income kept up with inflation. The real income of the lender, of course, goes down. When inflation isn't taken into account in nominal interest rates, some people gain, and some people lose buying power.

We will now study a phenomenon known as "The House Money Effect." The house money effect is a phenomenon in behavioral finance in which people are more likely to gamble with money they view as "extra" or "unearned" than with money they have earned themselves.

The term refers to a bettor who reinvests some or all of his or her winnings from an earlier bet.

When gains are considerable, individuals are more likely to take risks. The house money effect appears to diminish over time as the risk-taking propensity following gains diminishes.

The house money effect has important implications for financial decision-making, as it suggests that individuals may not always make rational choices when it comes to managing their money. It is important to be aware of this bias and to take steps to mitigate its effects when making investment decisions.

If buyers receive a windfall of money, like an inheritance or a big raise, the house money effect may cause them to take on more debt or buy a more expensive home than they had planned. This can increase demand for more expensive homes and raise housing prices in some places.

If a seller has recently made significant improvements to their home or has seen significant price appreciation, the house money effect may cause them to believe their home is worth more than it actually is. This can result in higher asking prices and contribute to overall price inflation in the local real estate market.

The house money effect, in general, can add to increased volatility in real estate markets because buyers and sellers may be more prone to taking risks or making choices based on emotion rather than logical and reasonable analysis of market conditions.

A similar phenomenon is the "Free Money Effect." The "free money effect" is a psychological phenomenon in which people tend to spend more freely when they believe they are not spending their own money but rather receiving it for free or through unanticipated windfalls.

If individuals start spending more than they earn and getting into debt as a result of the "free money effect," then that's a problem. Even after experiencing a financial windfall, individuals should not lose sight of their long-term financial objectives and priorities.

There are multiple ways in which the distribution of free money, such as payments made under the stimulus package or subsidies awarded by the government, can influence the real estate market.

First, an increase in real estate demand may result from the availability of free money, which may increase the purchasing power of prospective homebuyers. As a result, real estate prices might go up if desire is high.

Second, property proprietors can be encouraged to make improvements by the prospect of receiving free money. Homeowners may be encouraged to invest in their properties by offers of financial incentives, such as tax credits for making energy-saving changes or grants for remodeling.

Free money can have a short-term effect on the real estate market, but this effect can be fleeting. There is a risk that the market will revert to its prior level if the current flow of free money is not maintained.

Factors like the status of the economy, the level of interest rates, and regional market tendencies can all moderate the effect of free money on the real estate market. Therefore, these considerations should be included in any analysis of free money's effect on the property market.

As a result of the coronavirus outbreak in the United States, many companies and organizations had to shut down, events had to be canceled, and remote workers were encouraged to stay at home.

The "dash for cash," or the desire to hold deposits and only the most liquid assets, caused havoc in financial markets and threatened to make an already dire situation much worse as a result of the sharp contraction and profound uncertainty about the course of the virus and economy. To mitigate the economic fallout from the pandemic, the Federal Reserve took a number of measures to keep credit moving. Loans were made to help households, businesses, financial market participants, and municipal governments, and the government purchased a lot of its own mortgage-backed securities.

The Federal Reserve initiated a large-scale program utilizing emergency powers on March 15, 2020, in order to stabilize a turbulent economy under duress from the novel coronavirus COVID-19.

Chief among these emergency measures is the effective reduction of interest rates to zero and the 700 billion dollar round of quantitative easing.

Despite these measures, stock values plunged to their lowest point since Black Monday in 1987, and it is still unclear whether sufficient liquidity has been injected into the market to prevent widespread failures in the financial system.

The US housing market was severely affected by the COVID-19 epidemic. Here are a few of its effects on the industry:

Demand for homes has changed. Many people started placing a higher value on having a bigger home or one with more outdoor space as a result of remote work and lockdowns. As a result, there was a rise in interest in homes in the suburbs and countryside, while people were less interested in renting flats in the city.

There was a shortage of inventory in some

marketplaces because many homeowners decided against selling their homes during the pandemic. Because of this, home prices continued to rise, and rivalry among buyers became fierce.

Historically low mortgage rates: as a result of the pandemic, many people were able to affordably purchase a house for the first time. There was a multiplicative effect on the property market because of this.

As a result of lockdowns and supply chain disruptions, new home building slowed down, adding to the already dire housing shortage.

There was a rise in the number of real estate deals that were made online due to the prevalence of social distance policies. Some examples of this are remote closings and virtual house tours.

Some real estate markets in the United States saw substantial growth, while others experienced inventory shortages and economic uncertainty as a result of the pandemic.

When the housing market and home prices shift, it can have far-reaching effects on the industry as a whole. The following are some of the ways:

Impact of wealth: When the value of a person's house goes up, so does their net worth. Homeowners who have seen their wealth grow may find it easier to make big purchases as a result. To some extent, the economy could benefit from this uptick in expenditure.

As the demand for new homes rises or falls, the building industry can feel the effects of the housing market. A robust housing market can encourage builders to ramp up home construction, which in turn can generate new employment and fuel economic expansion. When the housing market is down, on the other hand, building firms may reduce their output, which in turn reduces demand and puts people out of work.

The state of the property market can also have an effect on consumers' outlook. A rise in home values can boost consumer confidence, which in turn can boost spending on other goods and services. In contrast, a drop in home values can make consumers nervous, leading them to reduce their outlays and dampen economic development.

The mortgage market has a sizable effect on the mortgage market. Higher home values can encourage more people to apply for mortgages, which in turn can boost lending and the economy. If housing values drop, however, lenders may be more hesitant to extend credit, dampening economic expansion.

Rising home prices are one factor that contributes to

rising family debt. Homeowners may be more likely to take out loans using their property as collateral if its worth rises. However, if home prices drop, many people will have more mortgage debt than their houses are worth. This can cause defaults and economic instability.

There can be widespread ripples throughout the economy that are triggered by fluctuations in the housing market and home values.

THE GREAT FEDERAL RESERVE REVERSAL

The Federal Reserve has been reducing the size of its balance sheet since March 2022. The Federal Reserve has decided to stop buying new securities to substitute maturing bonds, reducing its bond portfolio by about 95 billion dollars per month (only about 1% of its holdings each month) as of September 2022. At around 8.5 trillion dollars, the balance sheet is still sizeable despite being down by less than 6% from its all-time maximum in April 2022.

Quantitative tightening refers to the Federal Reserve's practise of "unwinding" its balance sheet (QT). Bill Merz, head of capital market research at U.S. Bank, said the following in response to the new decision, "This means the Fed is putting less liquidity in the market, which means other investors will need to create demand for bonds. Bond yields may rise slightly if inflation stays a concern and the

Fed reduces the amount of bonds it owns."

Over the next five years, you can expect several important trends that were sped up by the COVID-19 pandemic to start having lasting effects on real estate and land use. Many of these trends will affect the demand and supply in regional housing markets. Whether it's because of new technologies, changing demographics, the state of local job markets, or the rise of remote work, the list of the hottest housing markets in 2027 may look a little different than a similar list from today.

Fewer buyers, lower prices, and higher interest rates are what most experts in the housing market expect to see in 2023. As a result of price hikes and a lack of inventory, many would-be buyers have been forced to sit on the margins. The market value of a home could go down, but probably not as much as it did in 2008. There are those who think the property market will keep on performing better than it did before the pandemic.

US News and World Report forecast that the property market will enter a shallow recession that will end and begin again in 2023. It is assumed that by 2024, inflation will be under control, enabling mortgage rates to remain stable. Homes prices would increase but at a more gradual rate than in recent years. The Zillow Group also made forecasts for the property market in 2023.

Housing affordability is anticipated to increase marginally, which is a positive trend. Monthly mortgage payments that are too expensive and a lack of inventory will remain obstacles, but the market may be stabilizing.

First-time purchasers, who have had it rough in recent years, may find this encouraging. Zillow also forecasts that home prices will continue to increase, albeit at a more modest rate. Many things could be at play here, including a rise in interest rates, an increase in available inventory, and a slowing in the rate of employment growth. This could make it harder for some buyers to get approved for a mortgage, but it could make it easier for others to locate a house within their price range. (Santarelli, 2023)

Chapter Three
The Golden Rule of Real Estate Cycles, 2008-2026

"History doesn't repeat itself, but it does rhyme."

-Howard Marks, Mastering the Market Cycle: Getting the Odds on Your Side

Dr. Homer Hoyt (1895-1984) was an American economist and real estate expert who contributed significantly to the study of urban development and real estate market cycles. Perhaps he is best known for developing the real estate cycle, which defines the cyclical pattern of growth and decline in real estate markets.

The focus of Hoyt's research was the connection between real estate and the broader economy, including employment, population growth, and infrastructure development. Among his influential works on the subject are "One Hundred Years of Land Values in Chicago" (1933) and "The Structure and Growth of Residential Neighborhoods in American Cities." (1939).

Hoyt was a pioneer in urban planning as well, advocating for the use of zoning regulations to govern development and promote efficient land use. Throughout his career, he advised numerous cities and organizations, and his contributions continue to influence urban planning and real estate research.

Beginning between 1934-1940, Dr. Hoyt worked for the Federal Housing Administration, where he developed a method to evaluate which areas of cities were ideal for investment by mapping a city's housing stock using various economic and social indicators (housing age/value, race of tenants, owner occupancy, overcrowding, etc.).

These experiments led to the development of Sector Theory, also known as the Hoyt model, which posits that urban growth occurs along transportation arteries and that zones are not inflexible and can interconnect.

Real estate markets are cyclical, and a real estate investor must comprehend the current state and future direction of the market. The cycles of the real estate market consist of four stages: recovery, expansion, hyper-supply, and recession.

These real estate cycles are quite intricate; it is essential to remember that they are occurring simultaneously. Even though the national economy is robust, there may be a decline in real estate sales in certain areas.

The best part is that regardless of your current real estate phase, you still have the opportunity to succeed, particularly if you are willing to commit to your next real estate investment for the long haul.

Researchers have found that the average duration of a real estate cycle is between 10 and 18 years. Others have hypothesized a seven-year real estate rotation. However, it's not always easy to tell which will last the longest. These cycles can be greatly shortened by some variables and lengthened by others. It's worth noting that the present cycle is the longest one in the last 60 years.

The preceding discussion should have made it clear that real estate cycles have a major effect on economic indicators like jobs and wage growth.

Employee morale suffers, and people are sometimes compelled to relocate further from their jobs when they cannot afford to purchase in the area where they work. For companies, this is a bad occurrence because it drives up the price of transportation. Reduced savings and investment in equities and bonds will also hurt the economy.

When individuals spend more money on transportation, it means they have less disposable income to spend at local restaurants and shops. The economy is a complex system, but the old adage "out of sight, out of mind" holds true.

The four potential phases of the real estate market are described below.

A. Recovery:

- Oversupply of real estate on the market
- Prices and rentals are decreasing.
- Demand is decreasing.
- Time on the market increases dramatically
- The new development is overpriced and inert.
- Joblessness reaches its peak.
- People in the construction industry have difficulty working.
- Increasing foreclosures by banks
- Investment property values fall to their lowest point during each of the four cycles.

The recovery phase is also known as "Buyer Phase 1." This is a wonderful time to purchase, as prices are very low and things are beginning to rise. The longest stage of the cycle is the recuperation phase.

B. Expansion:

- Absorption of surplus production by the market.
- Time on the market falls.
- Employment growth rises
- Existing properties are undergoing renovations.
- Investment properties are at their lowest point but are beginning to rise gradually.
- Rental rates are at a record low and have begun to steadily increase.

As the number of bank foreclosures falls, competition is intense.

This phase is typically the best time to purchase, as you will have the shortest amount of time before prices begin to rise as we enter the next phase. During the recovery phase, supply slows but remains high, and the unemployment rate declines sharply from its peak. Attempting to time the market and purchase at the extreme bottom, as you might during a recession, is difficult and carries a high degree of risk.

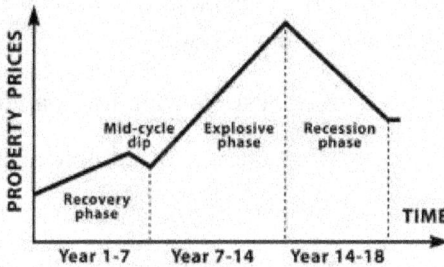

When these cycles occur in real time, it is difficult to determine whether you are at or near the absolute lowest pricing. This implies that these cycles could last a decade from the time of purchase while prices continue to decline.

Purchasing real estate during the expansion phase does not provide the same appreciation margin as purchasing at the absolute bottom. Still, it does provide a respectable risk-adjusted return. To take advantage of the market's upward momentum at a reasonable price, it's best to enter it during its expansion period.

C. Hyper Supply:
- The number of available properties on the market decreases

- Properties are selling quickly, and days on the market are at a record low
- After a lengthy lull, speculation and development are in full motion
- Low unemployment rate
- Rising property values and rents
- The demand for real estate is at its peak
- This is the phase of the real estate cycle in which investors receive the highest prices for their properties, and it is the worst time to buy.

At this time, it is best to wait for matters to calm down before engaging. Instead, it is preferable to concentrate on which markets and properties you wish to invest in once greater opportunities become available in the subsequent few cycles.

D. **Recession:**
- Time spent on the market begins to extend.
- The number of available properties increases.
- Sellers are still receiving inflated prices despite extended waiting periods.
- The land is being acquired for speculative purposes.
- There is an excessive quantity of construction in the pipeline, and overbuilding is likely.
- The demand for construction materials and supplies is increasing.
- Consequently, construction and material costs increase.
- The expansion of business and employment begins to decelerate.
- Rent expansion is stifled.

The recession phase is also known as "Seller Phase 2." This is the starting point for the values of real estate in the economy, and it presents the most significant opportunity to purchase foreclosed or otherwise distressed property at prices that are only a few pennies on the dollar. We will now discuss an economist who has been pivotal in the work of land reform.

THE REAL ESTATE CYCLE RESEARCHERS

Fred Harrison is a British economist and author who is best known for his work on land economics and the role of land in economic cycles. Harrison's main argument is that economic cycles are driven by land speculation and the increase in land values that accompanies it. He contends that as land values rise, they create a boom in the economy that eventually leads to a bust when the speculative bubble bursts. According to Harrison, this pattern has repeated itself throughout history and will continue to do so until the root causes of the problem are addressed.

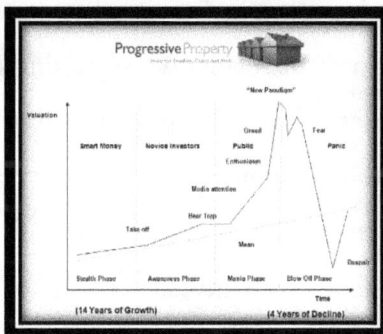

Phil Anderson has been studying economics and markets for more than 25 years at this point. And he can state categorically that the real estate cycle in Western economies lasts 18.6 years. On average, this fluctuates 14 years up and 4 years down.

A study of US history, for instance, reveals a very distinct (average) 18.6-year cycle in US real estate prices, as measured from bottom to bottom or peak to peak. The actual cycle length has never been less than 17 years or greater than 21.

According to Phil's research, the economies of Australia, the United Kingdom, and other Western nations follow the United States' main market movements, whereas, in Australia, each state experiences distinct fluctuations in between.

Phillip J. Anderson's 18.6 real estate clock is a fascinating tool that provides insight into the cyclical nature of the real estate market. The clock has twelve indicators that represent the various stages of the market cycle.

At the top of the cycle, we see rising interest rates, falling stock prices, and falling commodity prices. This period is marked by a tightening of the money supply and a reduction in overseas U.S. dollar reserves. It is a time of uncertainty for real estate investors as they brace for the inevitable downturn.

As we move further into the cycle, we see falling real estate prices, which can create a buying opportunity for those with the means to invest. This is followed by falling interest rates, which can lead to an increase in borrowing and stimulate demand for real estate.

Rising stock prices and rising commodity prices are also indicators of a growing economy and a potential upswing in the real estate market. Foreign exchange rates are another important factor to consider, as they impact the value of investments in foreign markets.

Finally, as central banks loosen their monetary policies, we see a rise in real estate prices and the potential for another boom cycle.

Overall, while Harrison's graph was an important development in the study of real estate cycles, Phillip J. Anderson's 18.6-year real estate clock represents a superior update that provides a more comprehensive, intuitive, and adaptable tool for understanding real estate markets.

The "18.6 formula" is a rule of thumb used by some real estate professionals to estimate the length of the real estate cycle, which is the period of time between the peak and trough of the market.

Who is Dr. Glenn Mueller? Dr. Glenn Mueller is a

real estate economist and professor at the University of Denver's Burns School of Real Estate and Construction Management. He is known for his research on commercial real estate cycles and his creation of the Real Estate Cycle Charts that track the performance of the four major property types in more than 50 metropolitan markets across the United States.

In the world of real estate, the concept of a "cycle" has been a topic of much debate and discussion. However, it was Dr. Glenn Mueller who revolutionized our understanding of this phenomenon and, in doing so, became a true pioneer in the field. Through his groundbreaking research, Dr. Mueller was able to reveal the underlying mechanics of the real estate cycle and how it is driven by both physical and financial factors.

Some critics argue that Dr. Mueller's focus on physical and financial factors may overlook the impact of other variables, such as technological disruption, demographic shifts, and changes in consumer behavior. Additionally, there may be opportunities to incorporate more soft data points.

The formula states that the length of the real estate cycle is approximately 18 years and 6 months, which is derived from the average length of past cycles. Specifically, the formula is based on the Kuznets Curve, which is a theory that suggests that as an economy develops, income inequality initially increases and then decreases over time.

On average, each 18.6-year cycle consists of 14 years up. Then subtract four years. Each 14-year increment can be further divided into two portions. Approximately seven years, with a mid-cycle decline or recession. The final two years of the 14-year period are known as the "Winner's Curse" The asset prices are overvalued and heavily leveraged by that point. This is not the time to be heavily leveraged and all-in.

The majority of economists and real estate experts surveyed by Zillow predict that home prices will increase by 46.5% over the next four years. A more conservative group forecasts a growth rate of 10.3 percent for the same period. In addition, only 8% of respondents anticipate that the housing market will favor purchasers substantially in 2026.

The 18.6-year real estate cycle is a concept that predicts that real estate prices tend to follow a predictable pattern over a period of 18.6 years. This cycle is composed of two main phases: the expansion phase and the contraction phase.

During the expansion phase, real estate prices rise steadily as demand for property increases. This is typically due to a combination of factors such as population growth, low-interest rates, and economic growth. As real estate prices rise, investors who own property can benefit from the appreciation of their assets, which can lead to significant wealth creation over time.

During the contraction phase, real estate prices begin to decline as demand for property decreases. This can be caused by factors such as economic recession, rising interest rates, or oversupply in the market. While this phase can be challenging for real estate investors, it also presents opportunities to purchase properties at lower prices, which can provide a foundation for future wealth creation.

THE REAL ESTATE INDUSTRY DOMINOS

How does the 18.6 Real Estate Cycle impact the business companies that provide services for the Real Estate industry? The Real Industry has an integrated model of the companies that serve the housing market. The following companies are divided into the following categories:

*Mortgage Packers or mortgage brokers face a slowdown during the contraction phase of the real estate cycle. The housing market has always been unpredictable, and it was no different for mortgage brokers during the last two years. Many mortgage brokers were hit hard, and some had to file for bankruptcy to get out of the slump.

*Credit insurers face higher levels of risk during the contraction phase of the real estate cycle due to increased mortgage defaults. The economic downturn caused by the pandemic led to an increase in defaults, and many credit insurers may have to face the music.

*During the contraction phase, investment companies may shift their investments to other asset classes. Investment companies were hit hard, and the stock market bubble of 2022 created massive losses.

*Consumer finance companies face a slowdown during the contraction phase of the real estate cycle due to decreased demand for loans. Consumer finance companies, which offer loans and credit to individuals, have been struggling to stay afloat during the last two years.

*During the contraction phase, money center banks may be more cautious and tighten their lending standards to reduce risk. Money center banks, which are large banks that deal with national and international markets, have had a tough time during the last year.

The mismatch in short and long-term lending has created liquidity problems. The FDIC deposit insurance may have to be raised to 25 million dollars. Richard Werner's argument for "money creation" is a critical factor in successful QE tightening.

*Regional banks may be more affected by local real estate markets and may experience more severe fluctuations during the real estate cycle. The regional banks have heavy exposure to commercial real estate. Many office buildings are in need of refinancing over the next 3 years. The large institutional investors' depositors may create new bank runs that lead to bankruptcy.

*During the contraction phase, title insurers may face reduced demand and lower revenue. Title insurers, which offer protection to property owners against defects in their title, have been struggling during the last two years.

*New Home Builders are impacted by low sales and increasing inventories, and massive price reductions. The Home Builders can offer outstanding opportunities for buying new homes at the lowest possible cost. Many residential homeowners are stuck in a frozen environment of low-interest rates and high prices.

*U.S. automakers may see decreased sales during the contraction phase of the real estate cycle as consumers have less money to spend. In 2008, many auto makers faced bankruptcy from the loss of auto revenues.

*During the contraction phase, furniture makers may face reduced demand and lower revenues. The key metrics are the debt levels and reserves for a real estate crash.

*During the contraction phase, appliance and tool makers may face reduced demand and lower revenue. Appliance and tool makers, which are considered essential, have been hit hard during the last two years.

*During the contraction phase, the home improvement industry will suffer from lower sales and a drop in revenues due to the fact that there is less money available.

During the contraction phase, construction and engineering companies will be hit with the loss of workers and collapsing revenues. Companies that do not have Federal Contracts will face heavy losses from the real estate industry.

*The Federal Reserve may also adjust interest rates in response to the real estate cycle and use other policy tools, such as quantitative easing, to support the real estate market during the contraction phase. The presidential cycle may result in a reversal of the Federal Reserve policy.

How do you prepare for the recovery after the crash of 2026? What steps do I need to take? Why is artificial intelligence an important part of the recovery process?

THE GREAT AMERICAN RECOVERY

The recovery phase of the 18.6-year real estate cycle is a time of great opportunity for those who approach it with the right mindset and strategies. With these guideposts in mind, we can navigate this phase with confidence and skill, ensuring that we make the most of the opportunities that present themselves.

First and foremost, it's crucial to stay informed about the state of the market. This means keeping up with industry news, monitoring trends, and staying abreast of local and national economic indicators. By doing so, we can position ourselves to make informed decisions about when and where to invest.

Of course, building up savings is also key to making the most of the recovery phase. This means living below our means, savings as much as we can, and being mindful of expenses. With a strong financial foundation, we can take advantage of opportunities as they arise without having to worry about stretching ourselves too thin.

Patience is also key. In the recovery phase, it's important not to rush into investments or make rash decisions. Instead, we should take the time carefully evaluate each opportunity, weighting the potential risks and rewards.

When evaluating investments, it's important to look for value. This means seeking out properties that are undervalued, have strong potential for appreciation, or offer significant rental income potential. By focusing on value, we can maximize our returns and build wealth over time.

Diversifying our investments is also important, as it helps spread our risk and protect us against potential downturns. This may mean investing in different properties or diversifying across different geographic regions.

Low-interest rates are another key advantage of the recovery phase, as they can make it easier to secure financing and increase our buying power. By taking advantage of these rates, we can stretch our dollars further and increase our returns.

When investing in real estate, it's important to focus on cash flow. The critical component is the cash flow from properties. Residential properties must "pencil out," whereas rental income must be greater than the mortgage payment.

Partnerships can also be valuable in the recovery phase, as they allow us to pool our resources and expertise with others. By working with partners, we can leverage our strengths and minimize our weaknesses, ultimately increasing our chances of success.

Building relationships with professionals is also important, as they can provide valuable guidance and support throughout the investment process. This may include real estate agents, lawyers, accountants, and other experts who can help us navigate the complexities of the market.

The great technology game changer is going to be Artificial Intelligence." Those who use the various AI platforms will have a competitive advantage. Real Estate will be the new race of A.I. applications. This critical technology will make a difference in Superforecasting the future. We call this the new Superforecasting tool of AI Real Estate 2.0.

Finally, it is important to remain flexible and adaptable in the recovery phase. Markets can be unpredictable, and being willing to pivot and adjust our strategies as needed can help us stay ahead of the curve and maximize our returns.

By understanding and tracking the 18.6-year Real Estate Cycle, investors and consumers can make more informed decisions about when to buy, hold or sell real estate assets. They can avoid industries that will result in high unemployment and long-term career instability.

This can help to maximize returns and minimize risks, which are both important factors in building long-term wealth through real estate investing.

Chapter Four

The Fall of the American Dream

In 2005, of the mortgages in Detroit, 68% were subprime. As the crisis cut a swath across America, 65,000 homes in Detroit were foreclosed.

Adam Tooze, Crashed

Anyone who has the misfortune of needing a mortgage is seeing the cost of housing steadily increase as interest rates continue to rise. Sellers are also wary of the market right now, which has a chilling effect on the supply of available houses.

High-interest rates are making prospective buyers nervous, which is reducing demand. Consequently, house prices are falling, but the expense of homeownership remains high.

Real estate prices have risen dramatically over the past few decades. Several factors, including shifts in the economy, have added to steadily rising construction prices.

There has been no letup in the current upward trend of home values. New York Rent Own Sell reports that home values have increased by 15% in the last 12 months. High housing costs are a direct result of the market's supply and demand situation.

When the COVID-19 pandemic first broke out, interest rates were lowered to stimulate the economy. Increased demand can be attributed to the dramatic decline in interest rates, as well as the fact that many Americans are looking to move out of expensive urban regions and into more affordable suburban settings.

However, numerous sellers pulled out of the market because of the uncertain economic and political climate. Since then, there has been a greater influx of buyers into the real estate market than sellers, driving up home values across the entire market.

In the past, the Federal Reserve kept the federal funds rate at 0.25 percent for a long time because there wasn't much inflation, and home prices were pretty stable.

During the pandemic, the government's loose loan rules sent billions of dollars into the economy. This made home prices unstable and led to a bubble. Lending institutions and investors took advantage of how easy it was to get loans. Investors started buying homes to flip, and banks gave money to almost everyone who asked. When these things were added to an already tight housing market and problems in the supply chain," housing prices went through the roof.

THE COLLAPSE OF THE AMERICAN DREAM

Many people's idea of the American dream includes buying their own homes. Some people make their living off of the outcome of a business choice. Everyone who has been in the market for a new home has run into trouble keeping up with the price increases in the real estate market.

The government's attempts to subsidize the cost of housing have not stopped the sharp increase in home prices in the United States.

In most cases, an individual's ability to make monthly mortgage payments is a deciding factor in whether or not they purchase a home. People spent more than the asking price, and bidding wars made it harder for the average person to buy a home.

As a result of the pandemic, a lot of people moved out of cities, which had an effect on regular market activity. Also, some businesses started offering work-from-home alternatives.

This meant that people didn't have to live close to where they worked anymore. Furthermore, some buyers were investors who planned to rent the properties that they purchased in order to generate passive revenue for themselves.

The typical American's purchasing power has been

eroded by rapid inflation since the Federal Reserve raised the federal funds rate, which increased the cost of borrowing money.

When the interest rate on mortgages went up, it stopped a lot of people from investing. As the pandemic has progressed, many individuals have already relocated. When you add these things to higher interest rates, there are fewer home sales in the works.

THE MIDDLE-INCOME SENIORS

Over 11 million middle-income seniors aged 75 and up in the United States may not be able to afford assisted living by the year 2033, and they are also unlikely to qualify for Medicaid to cover their long-term care requirements.

In an update to their groundbreaking "Forgotten Middle" study, experts from NORC at the University of Chicago find that the number of middle-income seniors will grow by 7.5 million (89 percent) from 2018 to 2033. The study also showed that there will be a significant increase in racial and ethnic diversity among seniors, with 22% of this middle-income population being comprised of people of color by the year 2033.

According to a new study from the University of Arizona, millions of American homes may become unsaleable between now and 2040, or their senior-citizen owners may be forced to sell at significant losses.

The research concludes that many empty nesters and newly single members of Generation X will have a hard time selling their homes. The issue is that many members of Generation Z and millennials either cannot afford or do not want such large houses, preferring instead to live in more compact dwellings in more central locations, perhaps even with access to public transportation.

There may be a 15 million-home surplus by 2040 as a result of millennials' shift in home-buying habits, the research finds, with homeowners likely to have to sell their properties for well below market value if they can sell them at all. The research concludes that the majority of seniors will be able to sell their homes but that this process may become more challenging in less-central, less-accessible, and less-growing markets.

The prediction was made by Arthur C. Nelson, a professor of urban planning and real estate development at the University of Arizona College of Architecture, Planning, and Landscape Architecture, and released in a paper titled "The Great Senior Short Sale" in the Journal of Comparative Urban Land and Policy.

Nelson used those numbers to create a graph showing how the median age of residents would rise from 2018 to

2038. Using data from three age categories (those over 65, those between 35 and 64, and those under 35), he concluded that, while the majority of people over 65 in 2038 will own their homes, there may be fewer homeowners under 65 in 2038 than there were in 2018.

"There's the mismatch – if those over 65 unload their homes, and those under 65 aren't buying them, what happens to those homes?" he asks.

Nelson is cautious about overstating his results, claiming only that "millions of people" will be interested in purchasing the homes being sold by the baby boomer generation. "But the vast supply is so large, and the demand for them is going to be so small, in comparison, that there's going to be a real problem starting later this decade," he said.

According to Nelson, the phenomenon will likely become apparent over the course of the next few decades, with roughly half a million to one million households experiencing it each year. It may not have much of an effect in rapidly expanding cities like Phoenix or Dallas, where "growth will solve all kinds of problems," as he put it, but it will be significant in tens of thousands of suburban and rural areas, including some parts of Arizona.

"The people who own homes now in thousands of declining communities may simply have to walk away from them," he said. (Kyle Mittan, 2020)

Nelson said that if the government paid the cost of buying homes that can't be sold or might become that way, seniors who lost their homes wouldn't have to turn to federal programs for help. These programs cost taxpayers a lot of money, and Nelson said that the cost goes up even more when the programs have to be run in country or suburban areas where homes aren't likely to sell.

The decrease in housing sales also impacted thousands of workers who found jobs in the booming housing market. Many of those who earned their livelihood through the business of real estate found it challenging to cope with the sudden fall in house sales as their jobs were on the line.

The real estate industry's biggest names—RE/MAX, Redfin, and Wells Fargo—have all revealed thousands of layoffs in recent months. Experts predict the reductions will ultimately equal those seen during the 2008 housing crash, which will have a devastating impact on workers across the board.

According to the National Association of Realtors, the number of homes sold in the U.S. dropped by almost 20% between August 2021 and August 2022. This was mostly because the Federal Reserve started raising interest rates in March to try to bring down inflation that had been high for decades. Because of this, mortgage interest rates have risen this year, making it harder and harder for people to buy homes.

THE COMING UNEMPLOYMENT CRISIS

"It's gonna be tough; layoffs are a common occurrence right now," said Linda McCoy, head of the National Association of Mortgage Brokers, who has been in the mortgage industry for 30 years. "It's scary because you just don't know where or when it's going to stop." (Pettypiece, 2022)

It's a big change from how the home job market has been in the past two years. As more people started working from home and interest rates fell to all-time lows, a lot of people started looking for new houses. Last year, there were more sales of already-owned homes than at any time since 2006.

During the first two years of the pandemic, when the job market was bad, the need for homes and the jobs that came from it was a bright spot. Analysts say that many of them wanted to move away from businesses like hospitality, food service, health care, and education that were hit hard by the pandemic.

However, two years following the pandemic, things

had changed starkly for workers in the real estate business. As the need for mortgage refinancing and home sales plummets, those who work in the mortgage business have been hit particularly hard.

Thousands of jobs have been lost in the mortgage industry over the past six months as over three dozen companies have either gone out of business, been acquired, or declared layoffs.

"We've had a frenzy, and it's come to a screeching halt," said McCoy, who runs a mortgage business in Mobile, Alabama. "It's going to be tough for those people that got in the business in the last two years that don't have a following already. I feel sorry for those people in a way because it looked like the best thing that ever happened to you." (Pettypiece, 2022)

The recent boom and bust in her industry, according to Lacy, who was laid off in July along with more than 300 other Sprout Mortgage employees, is reminiscent of the housing crash that started in 2007.

"Business was great. It was just how it was before in 2006; that's how busy it got. But now it just came to almost a screeching halt," Lacy said. "Beginning of the year, I started seeing those signs, and it was like, oh god, here it comes again." (Pettypiece, 2022)

Due to recent layoffs in her field, she is having trouble finding work. She hopes to pursue additional training in order to switch careers at the age of 43, possibly into the healthcare or IT sectors.

During the hiring boom, Lacy saw a large number of people attracted to the industry by large bonuses and the promise of remote work, including her daughter and her daughter's classmates, who have been laid off and are struggling to transition to a new career.

According to Ken H. Johnson, a former real estate broker who now analyzes the real estate industry as an associate dean at Florida Atlantic University, real estate brokers have also been affected.

Even in the best of circumstances, it can be difficult for new brokers to make a living selling real estate full-time. Now that sales are slowly going down, he thinks that the number of realtors, which is around 1.6 million, could drop by as much as 25% over the next three to four years, just like what happened after the housing crash in 2007 and 2008.

It's not easy to disentangle the causes of the rise in structural unemployment, but it's conceivable that it's higher now than it was before the housing bubble burst. In the ten years since the start of the financial crisis, automation has sped up, making it harder for people to find work in manufacturing. There is more competition from foreign manufacturers, especially in China.

The housing market crash and the subsequent decrease in the output of certain goods and services followed a predictable regional pattern. For example, Nevada, Florida, Arizona, and California were especially hit by the housing bubble—accounting for more than half of foreclosures at the national level—while, say, Ohio and Michigan endured the manufacturing collapse, New York and Delaware hosted the rearranging of financial institutions, and Hawaii experienced diminishing tourism demand.

The term "rent control" refers to a set of regulations imposed by the government that cap the amount of money a landlord can charge to enter into or renew a residential contract. Municipal governments are the ones who typically pass rent control laws, and the specifics of each ordinance can differ greatly from one to the next. To keep housing expenses manageable for people with lower incomes, all of these measures have been implemented.

In the United States, rent regulation is uncommon. A 2019 report by the Urban Institute found that of the 182 towns in the United States with rent control laws, all are located in either New York, New Jersey, California, Maryland, or the District of Columbia.

Recent years, however, have seen a resurgence of interest in rent control, especially in cities and states where rising housing costs and flat wages have led to an affordability problem for middle-class families and retirees on a fixed income.

It is often argued that the high expense of living in New York City proves that rent control is ineffective. As of March 2022, the median monthly rate for a studio in Manhattan was 3,417 dollars (non-doorman) and 5,022 dollars (doorman). (TEAM, 2022)

By preventing unreasonable annual rent increases, "controlled" rents can ensure that some housing remains affordable for those who cannot otherwise afford a house at the going market rate or higher.

Chapter Five

The American Nightmare

"We came of age in an economic system that has repeatedly failed us: two recessions before we turned 40; a multi-decade housing crisis that is keeping many of us off the wealth-building elevator."

-Nick Lichtenberg "Get Ready for the Mindset Shift of 'Retro Capitalism'

The possession of great wealth and fame does not necessarily preclude one from making a financial misstep. Even individuals with significant financial resources are susceptible to committing significant financial errors, leading to their entrapment in a cycle of debt.

The renowned actor, Nicolas Cage, has attributed his substantial financial liabilities amounting to millions of dollars to a real estate cycle. Cage, who has been honored with an Academy Award, has identified this as the primary cause of his financial predicament. "I made an excessive investment in real estate," during an interview with "60 Minutes," Cage stated he was unable to exit the real estate market before it experienced a significant decline.

"I paid them all back, but it was about 6 million dollars. I never filed for bankruptcy," he said.

An essential takeaway from Nicolas Cage's experience is the significance of possessing a real estate crash blueprint. The reality is that the 18.6 Year Real estate cycle was the real problem.

THE DEMOGRAPHIC SHIFT IN THE WEST

As a result of high mortgage rates and an uncertain economy, home price appreciation has slowed the most in pandemic boomtowns such as Phoenix, Austin, Texas, and Boise, Idaho. Based on a new report from Redfin, a technology-driven real estate brokerage, this is the case.

The pandemic era saw a surge of remote workers relocating from high-cost coastal cities to more economical Sun Belt cities, such as Austin and Phoenix, which resulted in a corresponding rise in home prices.

Within the top 10 metropolitan areas that are experiencing the most rapid deceleration of price growth, Las Vegas, Boise, and Sacramento are included.

Among the metropolitan areas that experienced the highest influx of new residents in the year 2021, Phoenix, Austin, and Las Vegas were noted, and Phoenix, Las Vegas, and Sacramento all featured prominently in Redfin's compilation of the most preferred locations for those relocating from out-of-state.

Boise and its environs have experienced a high rate

of growth in the past several years, drawing in numerous new inhabitants from California. Prospective purchasers with ample financial resources contributed to a rise in residential property values in sought-after locales during 2021 and 2022.

Maggie Ruiz, a representative with Redfin in Austin, laments the fact that the widespread uptick in home buying has made living there unaffordable for many residents. She has also seen a marked decrease in the number of people moving to the area and the number of people buying homes as investments.

"Even though affordability is a concern, in many ways, we are in a buyer's market," said Ruiz. "Some first-time buyers finally have an opportunity to purchase a home without competing with out-of-towners and investors.

Because prices and rates are high, a lot of buyers are offering below asking price, negotiating with sellers on a rate buy down, or considering new construction because many builders are offering significant incentives, including rate buydowns, to offload their inventory." (Richardson, 2022)

The rate at which home prices are increasing is noticeably decreasing in areas with prominent technology industries, namely San Jose, California, and Oakland, California. And Seattle, which is all included in the top ten list.

The city of San Jose, which witnessed a decrease of 2% in the median price per square foot during the month of October, as compared to the 20% increase that it had seen in February, holds the third position.

In the Bay Area and Seattle, which are highly expensive housing markets, purchasers are particularly suffering from the impact of soaring mortgage rates and declining tech stocks compared to the rest of the U.S. The continuation of double-digit home-price growth is not feasible in the long term.

Five of the 99 cities with the most people have seen their price growth speed up. One is in the Midwest, three are on the East Coast, and one is in Texas.

In October, the median price per square foot in Albany, New York, went up 11.2% from the same time last year. In February, the price per square foot went up 2.8%. That is the biggest increase in prices of all the metros in this study. After that comes Bridgeport, Connecticut, where the price per square foot went up 7.5% in October, up from 4% in February, and McAllen, Texas, where the price per square foot went up 18.7%, up from 16.1%.

All five of the metro areas where price growth has sped up this year while the housing market as a whole has slowed down are cheap and have fairly stable local markets.

Four out of the five have lower median home costs than the rest of the country. (Bridgeport is the exception). During the pandemic, prices went up in those places, but they didn't rise as they did in much of the rest of the country, so there's not as much room for them to go down.

High mortgage rates hurt places like Albany and Milwaukee less than they hurt other places because the lower the price of a home, the less it costs each month to pay the mortgage.

THE REAL ESTATE CHAINING EFFECT

Over the past two years, real estate agents have been encountering a market where prospective homeowners were only willing to purchase a new property after they had sold their own residence and had the necessary funds; evidently, they were apprehensive that they might find themselves in a financially precarious situation if they lagged in making the sale.

The phenomenon of 'chains,' a term referring to a sequence of domiciliary transactions linked by the requirement of one of the parties to first sell a house in order to complete the acquisition of the subsequent one, has had a detrimental effect on the housing market.

Slow sellers, slow solicitors, and increasingly, online

estate brokers who can cause delays are often cited as weak links in property chains.

Due to the inherent nature of their operational structure and the services they provide to users, numerous such companies encounter problems when communicating with buyers and sellers during the transaction process - especially after an offer has been accepted on a sale and prior to the final exchange of contracts.

The increased fragility of the chains renders them more susceptible to disruption. It is suggested that some online or hybrid agents fail to exercise sufficient scrutiny and due diligence when accepting offers from buyers, thus potentially exposing the chain to an increased probability of failure.

In order to optimize their chances of achieving a successful sale, sellers can take a number of measures. Furthermore, one should solicit information from the prospective agent pertaining to their sales progression setup and assistance when having the property appraised. Will you be provided with a single individual who will ensure you remain informed at all times?

When selecting an agent, it is recommended to prioritize those with the most reputable records and the capacity to ensure that all prospective buyers have been properly scrutinized and assessed for their ability to make a purchase before agreeing to a sale.

It is imperative that the intermediary verifies evidence of financial capacity, is capable of determining a target exchange date, and can guarantee that searches and surveys are requested by the purchaser within two weeks of the transaction being assented to.

The lack of dependency on a chain of processes or events has various advantages. However, there are also certain disadvantages associated with this.

If the desired property is out of reach financially, an alternative solution may include obtaining a rental property or residing with family members. It is said that guests and fish should not be kept too long.

Additionally, leasing is not cost-effective. In the past, the cost of buying was usually lower than renting; however, the trend has shifted in recent times. Finding a new place to purchase goods can take an extended period of several months to over a year.

It is conceivable that residential property values might experience an increase during that particular period. Consequently, the appreciation in house prices and rental prices may outweigh the benefit of a reduced price for a chain-free transaction.

Ultimately, severing the link implies that one will be required to relocate twice: initially to a provisional dwelling and subsequently when they purchase their eventual abode at a later date. The additional remuneration for the removal service may necessitate further outlay for storage.

THE HOME EQUITY PARADOX

What is the home equity paradox? Why is home equity considered an awful investment that is unsafe, illiquid, and has a rate of return that is always zero?

First, we must confront the harsh truth: your beloved home equity is but a sly trickster, masking itself as a pillar of stability while concealing its true nature. Not only is your equity unsafe, but it's also an illiquid beast. Your home equity is a function of paying down the mortgage and the appreciation of the property.

When life throws you a curveball, when the storm clouds of misfortune gather above, your equity may just be out of reach.

Imagine standing before a towering bank, pleading for a loan against your precious equity, only to be met with a cold and callous response, "Come back when you can repay, my dear borrower, or better yet, don't come back at all."

Just when you need it most, your equity may slip

through your fingers like grains of sand. Physical or financial disabilities can render you helpless, unable to grasp the lifeline of borrowed equity. Denied access, you may find yourself in a downward spiral, watching helplessly as your dreams crumble.

The secret is to separate your equity from your home. You can reclaim control and enhance the safety of your investment. Tools such as home equity loans, lines of credit, cash-out refinancing, reverse mortgages, sale-leaseback agreements, and equity sharing act as financial gateways, allowing you to release your equity from your home.

The housing market crash also led to a decrease in market shares for home builders, who had to resort to selling houses at reduced prices.

Homebuilding professionals anticipate an even steeper decline in the market during 2023 due to the apprehensions caused by high-interest rates deterring potential buyers. (Olick, Homebuilders say they're on the edge of a steeper downturn as buyers pull back, 2022)

The rapid increment in mortgage rates has led to a reversal of the previously heightened ardor of homebuyers; apprehension surrounding their prospective investment and the macroeconomic stability has become a cause of concern.

The U.S. homebuilding industry experienced a significant boon as a result of the Covid-19 pandemic. The convergence of exceptionally low-interest rates and rising consumer demand for larger dwellings resulted in an unprecedented surge in demand in the housing market.

In just two years, there was a 40% increase in home prices, and homebuilders were unable to keep up with the demand. There was a decrease in sales in order to maintain parity. However, that period has come to an end.

"Buyer traffic is weak in many markets as more consumers remain on the sidelines due to high mortgage rates and home prices that are putting a new home purchase out of financial reach for many households," said NAHB Chairman Jerry Konter, a homebuilder and developer from Savannah, Georgia. (Olick, More homebuilders lower prices as sentiment falls for ninth straight month, 2022)

Builders have indicated that construction costs remain at a heightened level while the increased interest rates are negatively affecting their sector.

The increase in costs associated with land, labor, and materials has impeded the ability of builders to decrease prices; however, they are now being compelled to do so. Many builders have had to lay off their workers and employees as they were unable to retain them.

Since there are fewer and fewer homes being bought, Furniture Makers/Tool Makers/appliances also lost their jobs, giving rise to Cyclical Unemployment. The term cyclical unemployment is a type of unemployment that is caused by fluctuations in the economy, such as recessions and business cycles, resulting in a decrease in the number of employed people. (periods of economic decline).

Cyclical unemployment can be characterized by economists as the consequence of businesses not having sufficient demand for labor to hire all those searching for employment at a certain point in the economic cycle. When the demand for a particular good or service decreases, supply production can be duly diminished in response.

Since fewer resources are needed to maintain the same amount of output, a smaller number of workers tend to be employed. The company will be terminating the services of those workers who are no longer required, which culminates in their unemployment.

The incidence of bankruptcy among Real Estate Investment Trusts (REITs) is remarkably small. It is necessary that Real Estate Investment Trusts maintain the majority of their possessions in physical real estate properties or loans supported by real estate collateral.

It can be stated that real estate assets, in the majority

of cases, tend to increase in value over the passage of time, and with the capability of sustaining their worth, Real Estate Investment Trusts (REITs) are facilitated to liquidate their holdings in order to diminish debt obligations in critical circumstances.

Despite the fact that several shopping mall Real Estate Investment Trusts (REITs) were undergoing difficulty prior to 2020, the phenomenon known as the 'retail apocalypse' exacerbated the situation. The devaluation of malls has been precipitated by declining rental and occupancy figures in numerous locations.

The COVID-19 pandemic accentuated the already existing issues. The bankruptcy filings of CBL & Associates (CBLQ) and Pennsylvania Real Estate Investment Trust (PEI) constituted the culmination of events.

It is anticipated that the bankruptcy filing will not eliminate shareholders. However, it will significantly reduce the worth of their possessions.

It is expected that Artificial Intelligence (AI) will lead to a decrease in job opportunities for college-educated workers within the next five years. As technology progresses, tasks which were historically thought to necessitate a significant degree of education and knowledge will be able to be accomplished.

THE COMING AI UNEMPLOYMENT CRISIS

The potential for automation to reduce costs may result in the displacement of workers from certain industries. It is challenging to accurately ascertain the degree of this phenomenon. However, it is obvious that Artificial Intelligence will bring about a noteworthy transformation to the employment opportunities accessible to those with a college education. It is essential for individuals to be aware of recent advancements in Artificial Intelligence and to contemplate how their knowledge and proficiency can be utilized in a world wherein machines are becoming more capable of performing many duties.

Technologists have forewarned for years that adaptable, innovative AI will pose a threat to white-collar employment as robots replace experienced office workers whose jobs were once deemed immune to automation. In the most extreme scenario, analysts envision AI irrevocably altering the employment landscape. According to an Oxford study, 47 percent of U.S. jobs may be at peril. (Lowrey, 2023)

Dr. Kai Fu Lee, a prominent figure in the AI industry, has been warning of a cycle of displacement and retention in the coming years due to advancements in artificial intelligence. His venture capital firm, Sinovation Ventures, has invested in 80% of AI companies that are expected to replace blue and white-collar workers.

One such company is UiPath, a robotic process automation firm that is already figuring out how to replace 70% of entry-level jobs in accounting and human resources. The impact of these developments is likely to be felt across multiple industries, with potentially disastrous consequences for those who are displaced.

According to Lee, this cycle of displacement and retention will last for the next 5-15 years, leading to widespread human depression, drug addiction, and alternative virtual reality games as people struggle to find meaning and purpose in their lives. Job growth will collapse with AI job replacement, which could take up to 25 years to fully take effect, and it take another 30 years before interesting and challenging jobs are created by AI technology.

This is not a distant, theoretical concern. We already see the effects of automation in many industries, with workers being replaced by machines and algorithms at an alarming rate. While some jobs will require human input, the number of available positions is likely to shrink, leading to widespread unemployment and social unrest.

What this would result in for the future of real estate

industry employees remains to be seen. However, the 18.6 Real Estate Cycle may create a "depression" era level of unemployment. How can AI solve some of these "New Deal" levels of unemployment?

*Job Matching: AI can be used to match job seekers with relevant job opportunities based on skills, experience, and qualifications.

*Skills Training: AI-powered training platforms can help workers develop new skills and knowledge, making them more competitive in the job market.

*Remote Work: AI-powered communication and collaboration tools can enable remote work, allowing workers to continue to be productive even if they are unable to physically attend work.

*Entrepreneurship: AI can be used to provide support and resources for entrepreneurs, helping them launch new businesses and create jobs.

*Job Creation-AI-powered analysis of market trends and consumer behavior can help identify new business opportunities, which can, in turn, create new job opportunities.

*Economic Stimulus: AI can be used to identify and target economic stimulus programs that can create new jobs and support workers during a contraction period. For example, President Biden could hold National Summit Conference for Community Colleges to design an AI national database of training programs and financial aid programs.

Chapter Six
The Real Estate Renegades

"76% of millionaires say anyone can become a millionaire with hard work and discipline."

- Chris Hogan, <u>Everyday Millionaires</u>

A dropping knife, or a falling stock, bond, or other security prices, presents unique challenges for investors. However, there exist certain individuals who possess a particular talent for accomplishing such a task. In this chapter, we will discuss the works of such people who have been pioneers in Real Estate; The Real Estate Renegades.

During the equity downturn caused by the credit crisis in October 2008, Warren Buffett authored an article in The New York Times op-ed section, announcing his purchase of American stocks.

The author's rationale for purchasing during times of market turmoil is based on the principle of contrarian investing, which advises individuals to exhibit caution when the majority of investors are exhibiting exuberance and capitalizing on opportunities when the majority of investors are exhibiting fear. Specifically, the author suggests that one should "be fearful when others are greedy, and be greedy when others are fearful."

Buffett excelled amid the credit crisis. He bought 5 billion dollars in perpetual preferred shares in Goldman Sachs (GS) with warrants to buy more shares at 10% interest. Goldman may repurchase the securities at a 10% premium. Buffett and the bank reached this accord in 2008. 2011 saw the bank repurchase the shares.

Buffett also bought 3 billion dollars of perpetual preferred shares with a 10% interest rate and redeemable in three years at a 10% premium from General Electric (GE).

He bought billions in convertible preferred shares in Swiss Re and Dow Chemical (DOW), which needed funding during the credit crisis.

Buffett has made billions and helped these and other American enterprises survive a challenging period.

THE BILLIONAIRE BOYS CLUB

John Paulson's credit crisis wager on the U.S. housing market made him famous. Paulson & Co. made 20 billion dollars from this crisis-time gamble.

He rapidly switched gears in 2009 to bet on a rebound and created a multi-billion dollar position in Bank of America (BAC) and around two million shares in Goldman Sachs.

He invested substantially in Citigroup (C), JP Morgan Chase (JPM), and a few other financial organizations and gambled large on gold.

Paulson's 2009 hedge fund returns were good, but he made tremendous money in big banks. He and his firm gained billions in assets and investment management fees from his credit crisis reputation.

Jamie Dimon leveraged fear to profit for JP Morgan during the credit crisis. Dimon bought Bear Stearns and Washington Mutual, two financial organizations that collapsed due to massive housing wagers during the financial crisis. JP Morgan bought Bear Stearns for ten dollars a share, 15% of its early March 2008 value.

It bought WaMu in September. WaMu's early-year value was similarly a fraction of the purchasing price.

Over 10 years, JP Morgan shares tripled from their March 2009 lows, making stockholders and its CEO wealthy.

Ben Bernanke, like Jamie Dimon, is not an investor. He led the Fed during a crucial time. The Fed's gutsy move in the face of uncertainty saved the U.S. and global financial systems, but it also benefited taxpayers.

A 2011 story reported 82 billion dollars in Fed profits in 2010. This included 3.5 billion dollars from buying Bear Stearns and AIG assets, 45 billion dollars from buying 1 trillion dollars in mortgage-backed securities (MBS), and 26 billion dollars from holding government debt. The Fed's balance sheet tripled from 800 billion dollars in 2007 to absorb a financial sector downturn, but earnings have improved since conditions have normalized.

Carl Icahn is a renowned fund investor who has demonstrated exceptional performance in investing in distressed securities and assets during periods of economic decline. The individual possesses specialized knowledge and skills in the acquisition of businesses, with a particular focus on companies operating in the gambling industry.

Previously, the individual procured three gaming properties in Las Vegas during periods of financial adversity and subsequently divested them at a substantial gain upon the amelioration of industry circumstances.

In order to demonstrate Icahn's proficiency in identifying market highs and lows, it can be observed that he divested himself of the three properties in 2007, yielding a return of roughly 1.3 billion dollars, which represents a substantial multiple of his initial investment.

Amidst the credit crisis, the individual in question resumed negotiations and successfully acquired the Fontainebleau property in Las Vegas, which had previously gone bankrupt. The property was procured for a sum of approximately 155 million dollars, which represents a mere

4% of the estimated cost of constructing the property. In 2017, Icahn successfully sold the incomplete property to two investment firms for a sum of almost 600 million dollars, thereby yielding a return of nearly four times his initial investment.

Maintaining a perspective amidst a crisis is a crucial distinguishing element for the aforementioned investors. A prevalent pattern among these individuals is their proximity to the centers of authority, as many of them fostered intimate associations with elected and appointed government officials and agencies that allocated vast sums of money, to the advantage of numerous major investors, throughout their professional trajectories, particularly in this era.

JP Morgan and the Federal Reserve are prominent and influential entities that individual investors cannot feasibly emulate in their personal investment strategies.

However, both entities provide valuable insights on how to capitalize on market turmoil. Once market conditions stabilize, astute investors may realize significant profits and those who can replicate their prior achievements during subsequent economic downturns may amass substantial wealth.

TOP THREE REAL ESTATE RENEGADES

The cinematic production titled "The Big Short," released in 2015, is a screen adaptation of Michael Lewis's eponymous literary work that achieved significant commercial success. The narrative chronicles the escalating predicaments in the American mortgage and housing sectors that preceded the Great Recession, as well as the select group of financial experts who not only anticipated the downturn but also successfully converted that forecast into substantial gains.

The present study aims to examine the phenomenon known as "the big short," including its underlying causes and the subsequent impact it had on the worldwide financial system. Additionally, this study will explore the biography of Michael Burry, a prominent conspirator, and how his prognostications yielded substantial profits for himself and his stakeholders amidst the deterioration of the worldwide financial milieu.

Michael J. Burry was raised in San Jose, California. The individual pursued a dual course of study in economics and pre-medical studies at the University of California, Los Angeles, subsequently obtaining a medical degree from Vanderbilt University School of Medicine located in Tennessee.

Following his relocation to California to pursue his residency at Stanford, Burry engaged in financial investing during his off-duty hours. The individual in question departed from his academic pursuits prematurely to establish his own hedge fund, which he christened Scion Capital.

Burry has said that his investment philosophy is based on the fundamental text for value investing, "Security Analysis," written by Benjamin Graham and David Dodd in 1934. He said: "All my stock picking is 100% based on the concept of a margin of safety."

Accordingly, by examining inflated businesses with little income or profitability, he was one of the first to predict the dot-com bubble. He started shorting those companies right away, and his investors swiftly saw spectacular returns.

Despite the S&P 500's roughly 12% decline in the first year (2001), Burry generated a return of 55%. Over the following two years, the market continued to tumble sharply, but Burry's fund generated returns of 16% (against a fall in the S&P 500 of 22% and a rise in the S&P of 50%), making him one of the best investors in the sector at the time.

Burry was so prosperous that organizations like Vanguard, White Mountains Insurance Group, and well-known investors like Joel Greenblatt expressed an interest in him. He was managing 600 million dollars at the end of 2004 and turning away investors as a result.

In 2005, Burry shifted his attention toward the subprime market. By scrutinizing the mortgage lending practices and bank balance sheets during the years 2003 and 2004, the individual observed noteworthy anomalies in this particular market. Consequently, the individual accurately anticipated the collapse of the housing bubble as early as 2007.

The individual observed the precarious nature of the subprime market, wherein a significant number of borrowers with limited income and assets acquired homes with substantial leverage. In numerous instances, these borrowers made no down payments for mortgages that would become unaffordable when interest rates inevitably increased.

However, the banking system was appraised at a value that assumed the mortgages to be entirely secure. Burry came to the realization that the long-term viability of the credit products, which were founded on subprime mortgages, was not feasible. He further observed that the value of these credit products would experience a sharp decline upon the replacement of the original rates with higher ones.

The aforementioned deduction prompted him to engage in a short position in the housing market by persuading Goldman Sachs and other investment banking firms to vend him credit default swaps (CDS) pertaining to subprime transactions that he deemed susceptible. In brief, recommend selling positions based on the premise that there will be a decline in housing prices.

Nevertheless, with the persistent escalation of prices, Burry's clientele became increasingly apprehensive and dissatisfied, while he persisted in his utilization of derivatives for his short positions. Regrettably or conversely, fortunately, upon reflection, Burry declined the investors' requests to withdraw their capital by imposing a moratorium on fund withdrawals, thereby exacerbating his clients' dissatisfaction.

Subsequently, Burry's analysis was validated when the market began to shift in the direction he had anticipated in 2007, as a greater number of insiders became cognizant of the inherent risks within the system. Subsequently, a chain reaction was initiated, leading to the collapse of Bear Stearns, Lehman Brothers, AIG, and other financial institutions.

Burry's investment yielded significant returns, resulting in a substantial personal gain of 100 million dollars and generating over 700 million dollars for his remaining investors. Scion Capital achieved a documented return of

489.34% from its inception on November 1, 2000, until June 2008. By contrast, the S&P 500 yielded a return of less than 3%, inclusive of dividends, during the aforementioned timeframe.

The film "The Big Short" chronicles the events that led to the 2008 financial crisis, which were primarily driven by the expansion of the subprime mortgage market and the associated investment instruments.

According to estimates, Grant Cardone is expected to have a net worth of 600 million dollars by 2023. He is a motivational speaker, author, and sales coach best known for his vast real estate business. He had to overcome many challenges along the way, but his tenacity and passion for business deals helped him become the successful entrepreneur he is today.

Cardone initiated his entrepreneurial journey with a consulting enterprise. The individual collaborated with automotive dealerships and manufacturers located in both the United States and Canada. The objective was to enhance their sales procedures to improve customer satisfaction, streamline operations, and increase profitability for both customers and dealers.

Grant aimed to cause a disruption in the automobile industry and, in the process, received financial compensation from the industry itself.

The individual provided consultation services while concurrently employed in the automotive sales industry until they accumulated sufficient funds to make a subsequent investment in the real estate sector.

During his tenure as a car salesman, Grant made an investment in real estate by purchasing a single-family property located in Houston.

Following a seven-month tenancy, the tenants vacated the premises. The individual experienced a cessation of their monetary inflows. This marks his inaugural instruction in the field of real estate.

The individual in question exhibited a preference for avoiding reliance on a single tenant as a sole source of revenue and financial liquidity. After a period of five years, the individual made the decision to acquire a multi-family complex located in San Diego as their next real estate investment.

One month subsequent to his initial acquisition of a multi-family property, he proceeded to purchase a second real estate asset. The individual's approach involved utilizing funds from the initial two sources to finance the third.

Grant persisted in employing this approach and gradually amassed an increasing amount of assets. As of

2012, it was reported that his enterprise had achieved the most substantial procurement of private parties in Florida, particularly for properties with multiple dwelling units.

Grant Cardone is the current proprietor of Cardone Capital, Cardone Training Technologies, Grant Cardone TV, and Grant Cardone Sales University, all of which generate multi-million dollar revenues on an annual basis.

According to reports, the companies under his ownership possess and manage investment properties valued at 800 million dollars within the United States.

The individual in question possesses a real estate enterprise valued in the millions of dollars, which spans various states, including Alabama, Arizona, California, Florida, Georgia, North Carolina, Tennessee, and Texas. Cardone Capital's growth and expansion are likely to be fueled by its motto of "Be obsessed or be average."

According to Cardone's statements in interviews, he possesses exclusive ownership of his holdings, with the exception of a minor portion of his real estate portfolio amounting to less than 2%, which is co-owned by external partners, including acquaintances and relatives. He maintains a close-knit circle of associates within his organization.

A significant portion of his investment portfolio is

funded through debt obtained from financial institutions and external stakeholders. The individual holds the belief that indebtedness can be advantageous and that currency serves as a means of exchange for personal liberty.

The primary source of Grant Cardone's net worth is attributed to his utilization of debt leveraging. The individual settles the outstanding balance by utilizing the earnings generated from monthly revenues.

Roy E. Carroll II has acquired a significant amount of land in the United States and has accumulated substantial wealth through investments in real estate and construction. Carroll, who serves as both the founder and chairman of The Carroll Companies, is a proficient entrepreneur and prosperous real estate developer.

His portfolio encompasses a range of commercial, residential, and industrial properties, with an estimated value of 2.9 billion dollars, as reported by Forbes. (https://www.legit.ng/business-economy/industry/1515730-roy-carroll-meet-college-dropout-owns-a-multi-billion-dollar-real-estate-empire/, 2023)

Roy's inclination towards the field of real estate was initially sparked by the intimate bond he shared with his father. Following his father's job termination, a household acquaintance provided him with employment to construct a dwelling.

Roy, who was enrolled in college at the time, collaborated with his father on the project. Following the conclusion of the class, he would offer his assistance in the manual labor of hammering nails and sweeping the floors.

Subsequent to the triumph of the aforementioned endeavor, the aforementioned individuals were commissioned by additional acquaintances to construct analogous projects.

Consequently, the father-son partnership resolved to establish a corporate entity and proceeded to erect approximately six residential properties on an annual basis throughout the 1980s. The father of Roy was responsible for overseeing and directing the work teams at the construction site, whereas Roy was tasked with managing the financial transactions and performing administrative duties in the office.

The pair achieved expedited construction timelines and enhanced client satisfaction by abstaining from utilizing bank financing for land procurement.

Consequently, their notable standing, characterized by effectiveness and excellence, was further strengthened. Roy acquired his father's 50% stake in order to expand the business into new subdivisions and has since operated as the sole proprietor.

Roy E. Carroll II has demonstrated effective leadership in the creation and management of a noteworthy real estate portfolio comprising residential, commercial, and industrial properties.

Chapter Seven
Maximizing opportunities

"There is no security on this earth. There is only opportunity."

-General Douglas MacArthur

Real estate investing success doesn't happen suddenly, and it certainly doesn't happen without careful preparation and execution. A real estate development business plan can act as a road map for entrepreneurs for all of their business activities. In other words, a real estate business plan will be crucial to shaping your investing career.

To construct a successful business plan, investors will need to strategically plan out a number of essential components. Future objectives, corporate ideals, financial plans, and other things are among them. Once finished, a business plan can lay the groundwork for efficient operations and chart a course for an investment career that has endless possibilities.

The real estate business plan is a dynamic document that serves as a blueprint for the objectives and operational framework of a business. A comprehensive business plan comprises a set of structured objectives for the organization's future and a well-organized strategy to achieve them.

Although there may be variations in business plans across investors, they generally involve forecasting for a period of one to five years.

Undoubtedly, one of the most crucial steps a novice investor can undertake is to formulate a business plan for the purpose of real estate investment.

THE SECRETS OF THE REAL ESTATE PLAN

Developing a business plan for REI can assist in mitigating potential challenges and concurrently positioning oneself for success. The blueprint serves as a guide to adhere to situations where events unfold as anticipated and in instances where they deviate from the expected trajectory.

The primary purpose of a real estate company's business plan is to provide investors with a clear roadmap to achieve their objectives. From various perspectives, there is nothing more valuable to contemporary investors. The strategy entails pursuing the most efficient route toward achieving success.

In its entirety, a comprehensive real estate business plan ought to encompass a firm's objectives in the near and distant future. In order to effectively communicate a company's vision, a comprehensive business plan necessitates a greater amount of information than a mere projection of future aspirations. A robust business plan for real estate investment should offer a comprehensive analysis of its intricacies.

The aforementioned components may encompass the organizational framework, monetary particulars, promotional strategy, and additional elements. When executed effectively, it will function as a thorough summary for all individuals who engage with your enterprise, regardless of whether they are internal or external stakeholders.

It can be argued that the process of developing a business plan for an REI venture demands a consistent and unwavering focus on meticulousness. Drafting a business plan for a real estate company may appear to be a challenging undertaking for novice investors, and indeed, it is. The key to success lies in the ability to discern the appropriate constituents to incorporate, as well as the optimal timing for their inclusion.

The vision statement of a company is fundamentally comprised of its mission statement and core values. Although not necessarily the initial phase of organizational planning, a well-defined vision statement is imperative for the triumph of a business venture.

The values of a company can serve as a guiding

force for making investment decisions and can also serve as a source of inspiration for fostering long-term partnerships with stakeholders.

It is recommended to align prospective employees, lenders, and potential tenants with the underlying motivations of your organization.

Prior to drafting your corporate vision, it is advisable to thoroughly consider exemplars that resonate with you, both within and beyond the domain of real estate. Can you identify a corporation whose values align with your own? Alternatively, are there any mission statements that you hold a negative opinion towards?

When devising a set of values for your organization, it may be beneficial to draw inspiration from the values of other companies. It is recommended that individuals seek feedback from their mentor or other network connections during the planning process. Primarily, it is crucial to consider the attributes that hold significance to you and their potential integration into your strategic business blueprint.

OUTCOME-BASED REAL ESTATE

Setting objectives is a crucial aspect of a prosperous business strategy. Goals are significant for a company as they not only establish a final objective but also delineate the necessary measures to achieve it.

Categorizing goals into short-term and long-term can be a useful approach. Long-term objectives generally delineate the strategic plans for the organization.

These may encompass preferred investment categories, profitability figures, and organizational magnitude. Short-term goals refer to the smaller and more specific actions that are necessary to achieve a larger objective.

An instance of a prospective long-term business objective is to secure four wholesale agreements by the culmination of the fiscal year.

The implementation of short-term goals can enhance the feasibility of the task by dividing it into more manageable and incremental stages. To achieve the objective of securing four wholesale deals, it is recommended to set some short-term goals.

These goals may include devising a direct mail campaign for the targeted market area, building a buyers list comprising 50 contacts, and finalizing the first property under contract. Deconstructing enduring objectives is an effective approach to ensuring personal responsibility, establishing time limits, and achieving predetermined aspirations.

SWOT is an acronym that represents the four key

elements of a strategic analysis, namely strengths, weaknesses, opportunities, and threats. Conducting a SWOT analysis entails a comprehensive assessment of one's organization and prospective rivals, wherein each of the four key areas is meticulously scrutinized.

The framework facilitates a comprehensive comprehension for entrepreneurs to evaluate the efficacy of their business operations and recognize plausible opportunities for enhancement. SWOT analyses are commonly employed in various sectors to develop feasible remedies for potential challenges.

In order to conduct a SWOT analysis for a real estate business plan, it is imperative to initially identify the potential strengths and weaknesses of the company. Do you possess tenants of superior quality? Do you encounter difficulties in acquiring funds? It is important to maintain honesty with oneself while categorizing the given information.

Subsequently, it is advisable to adopt a strategic approach by analyzing the market area and competitors in order to ascertain potential threats and opportunities. One potential concern pertains to the alignment of rental prices with those of analogous properties. Conversely, a prospective opportunity has the potential to enhance the amenities of your property, thereby increasing its competitiveness within the locality.

The implementation of a sound investment strategy is a crucial component of any effective business plan for real estate investment. Businesses may implement various exit strategies, such as rehabbing, wholesaling, and renting, among others, to ensure profitability.

Investors are advised to conduct a thorough analysis of their respective markets and evaluate the most suitable strategy that aligns with their objectives. Individuals with extended retirement objectives may wish to contemplate a significant emphasis on investment in rental properties.

Nevertheless, individuals lacking the financial resources to establish a rental portfolio may wish to contemplate commencing their investment journey through wholesaling. Regardless of the circumstances, it is imperative to determine the intended use for any property that is encountered at present.

It is noteworthy that the aforementioned approach will vary depending on the specific property. Consequently, it is imperative for investors to ascertain their exit plan predicated on the asset and their present objectives. The inclusion of this section in a real estate investment business plan is deemed necessary as it can prove to be advantageous upon identification of a potential investment opportunity.

There exist several variables that will exert upward or downward pressure on prices within the next two years, although they may exhibit a relatively stable trend until 2030.

It is plausible that a larger stimulus package may be implemented within the next five years. However, the national debt and trade deficit pose significant challenges that may impede unrestrained expenditure.

The prognostication of the housing market and the stock market is influenced by persistently elevated interest rates.

According to the current US Federal Reserve and government, the most effective approach to reducing inflation is through the implementation of consistently higher interest rates over a prolonged period of time.

Regrettably, the anticipated decline in home prices has not materialized, and the demand for homes continues to persist. The resurgence of inflation in January implies that there will be no immediate reduction in mortgage rates. It is anticipated that the years 2023 and 2024 will be characterized by the continued presence of inflation, followed by a probable period of stagnation.

The increase in M2 money supply is having a

detrimental effect on market liquidity, while the escalation of interest rates is rendering investment in housing less probable.

Based on current trends and projections, it is anticipated that the housing market will experience a moderate level of improvement by the year 2028. The current surge in home prices can be attributed primarily to the increase in immigration, as there is limited evidence to suggest any other significant contributing factors.

The forthcoming 2024 elections are poised to provide significant insights into the potential impact on housing demand pressures that may transpire in 2026.

In the absence of new housing construction, the decision to sell a home may not be deemed prudent, as sellers may encounter a lack of viable relocation options. The majority of individuals are unlikely to exhibit a high level of tolerance towards the ambiguity that may arise within the upcoming five-year period.

Given the current state of housing construction, it is projected that prices will remain elevated for a minimum of five years. The implementation of NIMBY (Not In My Backyard) and anti-development regulations by local government entities may result in a shortage of supply.

The dynamics of the market can experience rapid

fluctuations when the perception shifts from homes being assets with potential appreciation to those that may decrease in value. The reluctance to obtain a mortgage on a property that has the potential to decrease in value is a result of the possibility of reduced demand.

Oftentimes, predictions of negative outcomes do not come to fruition. However, if one desires to mitigate risk regarding a significant asset, it may be prudent to take into account demographic patterns.

A financial instrument known as a reverse mortgage is available exclusively to homeowners who are 62 years of age or older. This financial option enables the conversion of a fraction of the equity in one's residential property into liquid funds.

To be eligible for a reverse mortgage, specific requirements must be satisfied, such as possessing homeownership and possessing adequate equity.

REVERSE MORTGAGE AND AGING

A reverse mortgage has the potential to assist in debt repayment and provide increased financial security during retirement. It is crucial to obtain comprehensive information prior to affixing one's signature on the designated space.

In contrast to a traditional home equity loan or second mortgage, the borrower is not required to make loan repayments until they cease to utilize the property as their primary residence or default on the loan obligations.

Reverse mortgages are a financial product intended for elderly individuals who possess a pre-existing residential property. The property owners have either fully settled their outstanding debts or possess substantial equity, amounting to no less than 50% of the property's total value.

Reverse mortgages encompass a range of payment options, with the majority being classified as Home Equity Conversion Mortgages (HECM).

The loans in question are underwritten by the Federal Housing Administration (FHA). The Federal Housing Administration (FHA) upholds stringent criteria for reverse mortgages in order to safeguard the interests of both borrowers and lenders.

A reverse mortgage is a variant of a conventional mortgage, whereby the borrower receives a loan and is obligated to make monthly payments to the lender.

A reverse mortgage is a type of loan that allows homeowners to borrow against the equity in their homes. Monthly payments comprising principal and interest are absent. Consequently, the loan is transformed into periodic installments disbursed to the borrower.

The aforementioned funds may be allocated towards

discharging outstanding debts or financing necessary expenditures related to sustenance, such as sustenance and healthcare expenses. Typically, reverse mortgages are not utilized for leisure activities or other discretionary expenditures.

The monthly payments you receive from a reverse mortgage are often tax-free, to name a few points. A reverse mortgage shouldn't have an impact on your Social Security or Medicare benefits. Ordinarily, the loan is not required to be returned until six months have passed since the last surviving borrower died, sold the property, or ceased to occupy it as their principal residence.

Apartment Complex in Bankruptcy

The possibility of a landlord filing for bankruptcy is a daunting scenario that may potentially affect any individual. In the event that such an occurrence transpires, there is no cause for undue concern. The protection of tenant rights is robust in cases of landlord bankruptcy. In certain circumstances, it may be necessary to take measures in order to maintain one's tenancy in a given apartment.

In the event of an apartment complex owner's bankruptcy filing, all assets belonging to the owner are included in the bankruptcy estate. This encompasses all tangible assets, including the actual apartment complex.

The individual who owns the property and is commonly referred to as the debtor in the context of bankruptcy proceedings is provided with an inherent "stay" that serves as a legal injunction, thereby prohibiting creditors from pursuing debt collection from the debtor.

Furthermore, it precludes the initiation of any additional legal proceedings in which the debtor may be involved. The debtor is afforded a period of time to organize their financial affairs and devise a strategy for reimbursing their creditors.

The resolution of your lease will be determined during the bankruptcy process. The determination of whether to assume or reject the leases of an apartment complex in the context of bankruptcy proceedings is contingent upon the specific type of bankruptcy being pursued and may be made either by the landlord or a trustee appointed by the court.

If the lessor takes over the lease agreements, the commercial operations proceed without interruption. The lessees shall be obligated to remit rental payments to the lessor without any deviation, notwithstanding any intervening circumstances.

In the event of bankruptcy, landlords are permitted to undertake leases solely upon rectifying any pre-existing defaults and providing evidence to the court of their capability to fulfill their obligations under the lease.

Rejecting the leases is presented as an alternative to making assumptions. In this particular scenario, the lessor is absolved of any contractual responsibilities that were previously agreed upon in the lease agreement, including but not limited to upkeep and provision of essential services.

Tenants are presented with a binary option: vacate the apartment at their discretion, irrespective of the lease's specified termination date, or opt to stay in the apartment and fulfill their rental obligations.

In accordance with the lease agreement, tenants who choose to remain in the rental property have the right to deduct from their rent any expenses incurred as a result of the landlord's failure to fulfill their obligations.

In the event that the lessor or fiduciary assumes the lease agreements, they may subsequently elect to transfer the lease agreements to a third party. Under such circumstances, the third party obtains revenue from the residential complex and takes on the landlord's contractual duties as stipulated in the lease agreement.

In certain circumstances, the proprietor or legal custodian of a residential complex may opt to vend the property, typically via a public sale. Bankruptcy legislation allows for the unencumbered sale of assets, such as leases, without any obligations.

The decision to uphold the current leases lies with the prospective proprietor. It is probable that a new proprietor would find it economically advantageous to retain existing tenants, as this would ensure a consistent revenue stream from the outset.

In the event of an apartment complex declaring bankruptcy, the primary concern for residents may pertain to the status of their security deposit. The deposit is considered the property of the tenant, and any claims by the landlord's creditors are deemed invalid.

However, in the event that the landlord has utilized the deposit, the tenant may be required to exercise patience in awaiting their turn in the queue.

In the event of such a circumstance, it is imperative that you expeditiously communicate with the trustee by means of a written correspondence elucidating your entitlement to the funds.

In the event that the landlord is devoid of available funds, the trustee is granted the legal authority to liquidate any non-cash assets belonging to the landlord and distribute the resulting funds among the creditors. Priority is usually given to tenants who are owed security deposits over other creditors.

Yet, there are safe real estate investments that can be made during a contraction period of the 18.6 Real Estate Cycle. The Real Estate Cycle, also known as the "Kitchin Cycle," is a theory that suggests the real estate market experiences a cycle of around 18 years. During this cycle, there are periods of expansion, contraction, and stabilization.

During a contraction period, the real estate market experiences a slowdown in growth, and property values may decline. However, there are still safe real estate investments that can be made during this time.

One option is to invest in real estate investment trusts (REITs) that specialize in defensive sectors. Defensive sectors are those that are less impacted by economic downturns, such as health care and apartments. T These defensive REITs typically have stable rental income and may even benefit from increased demand during economic downturns. The (REITs) to avoid are mortgage, office and commercial, and retail.

NEW HOME SALES

The collapsing new homebuilder offers a unique opportunity for astute home buyers. They can offer once-in-a-lifetime opportunities. The key money-making strategy is to follow the North Star of real estate success. Why invest at the bottom of the market in 2026?

*New Homes offer lower prices, and this makes homes more affordable.

*New homes often feature modern designs and the latest features and technology, which can be appealing to buyers.

*New homes are likely to have fewer maintenance issues than older homes, which can save buyers money in the long run. Additionally, new homes may come with warranties that cover certain repairs.

*During the contraction phase, there may be more new homes available on the market as builders try to sell their inventory. This can provide buyers with a greater selection of homes to choose from, giving them more options to find a home that meets their needs and budget.

*While it may take time for the real estate market to recover from the contraction phase, new homes have the potential to appreciate in value over time. The 18.6 Year Real Estate Cycle creates 14 years of appreciation. This can provide buyers with a good return on their investment if they plan to sell their home in the next peak.

Another safe option is to invest in apartment properties that have long-term lease agreements with strong tenants. These properties provide a stable source of income, even during periods of economic uncertainty. Additionally, investing in properties with a low loan–to–value ratio (LTV) can also help to minimize risk.

Finally, investing in real estate crowdfunding platforms can provide access to a diversified portfolio of real estate investments. These platforms often offer investments in properties with lower minimum investments, making them accessible to a wider range of investors.

Chapter Eight
The Crash Blueprint

"A pessimist sees the difficulty in every opportunity; an optimist sees the opportunity in every difficulty."

-Sir Winston Churchill

Securities, referred to as "cash equivalents," are designed for short-term investing. They typically have excellent credit quality and are quite liquid. Since they may be rapidly exchanged for genuine currency, they are regarded as being equivalent to cash.

On balance sheets, the term "cash and cash equivalents" is used in the current assets section. One of the three main asset groups in investing is cash equivalents. Stocks and bonds make up the other two.

Securities with a cash equivalent have a low-risk, low-return profile. Cash equivalents comprise various money markets instruments such as U.S. government Treasury bills, bank certificates of deposit, bankers' acceptances, and corporate commercial paper. Financial instruments frequently possess brief maturities, remarkably fluid markets, and minimal risk.

Cash equivalents hold significant importance as a metric for assessing the financial health of a corporation. The feasibility of investing in a specific company can be evaluated by analysts based on the company's capacity to promptly access and convert cash equivalents.

The level of liquidity exhibited by a company indicates its capacity to meet its financial obligations. Enterprises possessing substantial cash and cash equivalents may serve as prime objectives for larger corporations with intentions of acquisition.

A money market fund is a financial vehicle that belongs to the category of mutual funds. Its investment strategy primarily focuses on low-risk, short-term debt securities and cash.

Money market funds are widely regarded as a low-risk investment option that generates income, typically commensurate with short-term interest rates. The tax implications of this income are contingent upon the specific investments held by the fund, with some generating taxable income and others generating tax-exempt income.

Similar to other types of mutual funds, money market funds construct a collection of securities and distribute shares to investors, who receive returns from the portfolio in the form of capital gains and income.

Money market funds construct portfolios consisting of various cash and cash equivalents, such as certificates of deposit (CDs), commercial paper, repurchase agreements, U.S. Treasuries, and bankers' acceptances.

Certain money market funds are tailored to cater to individual investors, whereas others are exclusively intended for institutional investors and necessitate substantial minimum investments.

Money market funds generate periodic income that may be subject to taxation or tax exemption, contingent on the nature of the security responsible for the income, owing to their investment in debt instruments.

Historically, money market funds have endeavored to achieve a net asset value (NAV) of 1 dollar per share. Any variance between the NAV share price and the returns generated by the portfolio's investments is allocated to investors in the fund.

Investments inherently carry the possibility of financial loss. Money market funds are commonly acknowledged as a highly secure, low-risk, and minimally volatile investment alternative.

Gold exchange-traded funds (ETFs) are comparable to mutual funds in that they are traded on stock exchanges, enabling investors to purchase and sell units through these exchanges. Similar to an equity mutual fund, an asset management company (AMC) collects funds from investors to invest in shares. However, in this case, the investment is made in pure gold.

THE GOLDEN FLEECE PORTFOLIO

Investors are allocated units by the AMC, which can subsequently be traded on exchanges. The exchange-traded fund (ETF) price exhibits a correlation with the physical gold that underlies it, thereby introducing the versatility of equity investment to the traditional gold investment.

Each unit of a Gold Exchange Traded Fund (ETF) symbolizes one gram of gold with a purity of 99.5%. The physical gold is securely stored in the vaults of custodian banks and serves as the underlying asset that determines the value of the units.

Exchange-traded funds (ETFs) that track the price of gold are subject to uniform buying and selling rates, unlike physical gold.

The pricing of physical gold exhibits regional variations across different geographic locations. The differential buying and selling rates are implemented to account for the expenses associated with the liquidation and other transactional costs involved in the physical gold trade.

Investing in gold is like following the footsteps of the legendary hero Jason and his crew of Argonauts, who sailed across treacherous waters in search of the fabled Golden

Fleece. Like these brave adventurers, gold investors set out on a daring quest to acquire this precious metal with the promise of untold riches and rewards.

With each investment in gold, it's as if the investor is adding a piece to their own personal golden fleece, just like the ancient Greeks who sought to capture the prized fleece of a magical ram. Each transaction is a treasure to be cherished and protected, building upon the foundation of the investor's portfolio and helping them to create a masterpiece of financial security and success.

Ancient miners would trap the smallest flakes of gold in the fleece by placing it downstream of a water flow. Just like these skilled miners, gold investors carefully collect every valuable opportunity, capturing each flake of gold and using it to weave a tapestry of financial prosperity.

As the fleece absorbs the gold flakes, the investor's portfolio absorbs the value of their investments, creating an imprint of financial success that shines bright like gold. The gold investor becomes like a master weaver, expertly crafting a tapestry of prosperity that is both beautiful and valuable, just like the golden fleece of legend.

Investing in gold requires skill, patience, and a keen eye for opportunity, much like the ancient miners who painstakingly extracted the precious metal. But for those who are willing to put in the effort, the rewards are worth the journey.

What is an example of investing in a real estate-driven recession? One financial planner offers a golden fleece scenario that will help you invest your money into different investment categories to diversify your portfolio and maximize your returns. We call this the "Golden Fleece Portfolio."

This portfolio is only for illustration purposes and is designed to demonstrate the value of recession investments. Let start with a hypothetical million-dollar investment which can be also be applied to 1,000 dollar investment.

First, let's consider investing 200,000 dollars into Treasury-only funds. These funds are highly secure and invest only in US Treasury securities, making them a low-risk investment option. They offer stable returns and are an excellent choice for conservative investors who prioritize safety over high returns.

Next, let's allocate 150,000 dollars to Money Market Funds. These Funds invest in highly liquid, short-term debt securities and offer low-risk, stable returns. They are also highly accessible, allowing you to easily access your funds when you need them.

From the remaining 650,000 dollars, we'll invest

300,000 dollars into US Treasury securities and savings bonds. These are government-issued securities that provide a fixed rate of return and are considered one of the safest investment options available. They are ideal for long-term investors who prioritize security and want to protect their capital from market fluctuations.

Next, we'll allocate 50,000 dollars to bank money market accounts. These accounts offer higher interest rates than traditional savings accounts and are insured by the FDIC, making them a safe investment option.

To add some diversity to the portfolio, we'll invest 75,000 dollars in gold stocks. Gold is a safe-haven asset that has historically retained its value during economic downturns. Gold stocks offer an excellent opportunity to invest in gold-related companies and benefit from their growth potential.

For 50,000 dollars, we'll invest in a Gold ETF, which tracks the price of gold and offers a low-cost way to invest in this precious metal. Additionally, we'll allocate 25,000 dollars to Gold Mutual Funds, which invest in a diversified portfolio of gold stocks, providing exposure to multiple companies in the industry.

To further diversify our portfolio, we'll allocate 25,000 dollars to Silver ETF and 25,000 dollars to Platinum

ETF. Silver and platinum are precious metals that have similar properties to gold and can serve as a hedge against inflation.

Finally, we'll invest 25,000 dollars in foreign currencies, specifically yen and euros. This helps us diversify our portfolio geographically and benefit from currency fluctuations. Yen and euros are major currencies that are relatively stable and have a strong track record of maintaining their values.

What are some major real estate categories that will be impacted by the U.S.A. real estate crash?

*Mortgage Brokers

*Credit Insurers

* Investment Companies

*Consumer Finance Companies

*Money-Centered Banks

*Regional Banks

*Title Insurers

*US auto makers

*Appliance and Tool Makers

*Property Developers

*Construction and Engineering Companies

*Non-Banks

These companies will experience massive disruption in their respective industries. Companies that have high debt and are heavily leveraged will have the highest chance of failing. The best way to research these companies is to find a stock market service that will research these companies. There are numerous stock research companies like VectorVest and Stock Market Almanac.

REAL ESTATE SUPER FORECASTING

During a real estate crash, investors often face a great deal of uncertainty and volatility in the market. However, the advanced AI algorithms used by Complete Intelligence's CI Future investment forecast can provide valuable insights and help investors make informed decisions in the face of such market turbulence.

Complete Intelligence, the AI Super forecasting company, is revolutionizing the way we approach investment forecasting with its cutting-edge technology and unparalleled accuracy. At the heart of their game-changing strategy is their flagship product, CI Future.

CI Future is an investment forecast that analyzes a staggering 1,200 stocks, currency pairs, commodities, and market indices, using advanced algorithms. They make their predictions with a one-year horizon and monthly intervals. The results? Faster, smarter decisions that take into account a mind-boggling 10 billion data points.

To say that CI Future is impressive is an understatement. This state-of-the-art investment tool has the potential to change the investment game as we know it. Gone are the days of relying on gut instincts or hunches. Instead, investors can now turn to the power of AI to make informed decisions that are backed up by real data.

During a real estate crash, many investors may be tempted to panic and sell off their assets in a bid to limit their losses. However, by relying on CI Future's data-driven insights, investors can take a more measured approach, assessing the market conditions and making decisions based on real-time data and analysis.

It's not just the technology that sets Complete Intelligence apart, though. The company's dedication to innovation and staying at the forefront of the industry is what truly makes it stand out. By continuously refining its algorithms and incorporating the latest advancement in AI, Complete Intelligence is constantly improving the accuracy and effectiveness of its investment forecasting tools.

Let's compare this with Jeffrey Hirsch Stock Market Almanac, 2023. This system has gained a reputation for providing timely and accurate market analysis, as well as profitable ETFs and specific buy and sell recommendations.

But what really sets it apart is its seasonal trade, including the January Barometer, Santa Claus Rally, and election cycles. These trades have been identified and analyzed with a fine-tooth comb, giving investors a leg up on the competition. And if that wasn't enough, the Almanac also includes price limits to help investors manage risk.

Now, let's turn out attention to Vector Vest, a system that has been in use for the last 30 years. This system relies on three mathematical models to create a statistically clear buy, sell or hold recommendation. These models include relative value, relative safety, and relative timing. By analyzing these factors, Vector Vest can provide investors with a comprehensive understanding of which stocks are worth investing in and which should be avoided. And if that wasn't enough, Vector Vest also includes an advanced portfolio analysis tool to help investors maximize their returns.

So which system is better? It ultimately depends on the investor's individual needs and preferences. The Jeffrey Hirsch Stock Market Almanac, 2023, is ideal for those who are looking for seasonal trades and specific recommendations. On the other hand, Vector Vest is better suited for those who prefer a more analytical approach, relying on mathematical models to guide their investment decisions.

In conclusion, both the Jeffrey Hirsch Stock Market Almanac, 2023, and Vector Vest are powerful tools that can help investors navigate the complexities of the stock market. By providing timely analysis, specific recommendations, and advanced portfolio analysis, these systems can help investors make informed decisions and maximize their returns. So whether you prefer a more analytical approach or seasonal trades, there's a system out there for you.

One of the major shorts of the real estate crash is the ETF DRV which gives investors 3x leveraged inverse exposure to an index of big-cap US real estate equities. The use of ETF DRV is used to give the investor more liquidity and allow for long-term participation in the 2026 real estate bottom.

The investment tries to get daily results, before fees and costs, that are 300% of the opposite of what the Real Estate Select Sector Index does daily. At least 80% of the fund's net assets (plus any money it borrows to spend) are put into swap agreements, futures contracts, short positions, or other financial instruments that give inverse or short daily exposure to the index or ETFs that track it.

The index is made by S&P Dow Jones Indices, and it includes securities from companies in the real estate management and construction industries, as well as REITs (real estate investment trusts) that are not mortgage REITs. The money is not spread out.

In the event of a potential collapse in the housing market, individuals may seek to capitalize on the situation for financial gain. How can one engage in the short sale of real estate?

Initially, it is imperative to ascertain the precise methodology for shorting the housing market, given the existence of multiple alternatives at one's disposal.

One strategy for making money from a home market crash is to short REITS. These businesses have large real estate holdings, so if home prices drop, the stock price will too. REITs can be sold short, or you can purchase or sell puts or calls in the options market.

You can also think about shorting REIT ETFs. There are several different REIT ETFs available, some of which have a narrow concentration on real estate. Either trade calls or put options, or consider shorting REIT ETFs.

Inverse REIT ETFs are another option that provides short exposure to real estate. If you come across any overleveraged REITs, you might want to think about selling them individually or simply purchasing an inverse REIT ETF.

Additionally, you should be aware that inverse ETFs, particularly leveraged ones, are risky financial instruments. Hence, approach this kind of trade with caution.

There are several businesses that would be appropriate to short the real estate market if you wanted to select particular equities to be short. These equities include well-known real estate players who are not REITs, like Redfin, Rocket Companies, and Zillow.

Another indirect method of shorting the housing market involves shorting businesses with large real estate holdings. Even if real estate is not their primary focus, there are many businesses that make significant real estate investments.

These businesses are a good fit because a collapse in the property market will probably result in impairment losses for their stockholders.

Real estate depended on companies are companies where at least 50% of their assets, gross revenues, or net profits come from real estate or activities related to real estate.

Real estate companies can be real estate operating companies, real estate investment trusts (REITs), or special purpose entities like pass-through trusts or other special purpose entities that issue commercial mortgage-backed securities (CMBS) and/or do real estate financings or securitizations. However, these are not the only types of real estate companies.

A fixed-income security is an investment that generates income through regular fixed-interest payments and eventual principal repayment at maturity. A fixed-income security's returns are known, in contrast to variable-income securities, whose payments fluctuate depending on an underlying variable like short-term interest rates.

A defined amount of interest is paid to investors in the form of coupon payments by fixed-income securities, which are debt instruments. The money is given back to the investor at maturity, and interest payments are frequently made every two years. The most popular type of fixed-income securities is bonds.

Bonds are financial instruments that are issued by corporations and governments to generate capital for financing projects and supporting ongoing gas operations. Bonds issued by corporations and governments exhibit a range of maturities and face values.

The nominal value of a bond, commonly referred to as the face value, represents the total amount that an investor will receive upon the bond's maturity. Bonds issued by corporations and governments are commonly traded on prominent exchanges and are typically denominated with a face value of 1,000 dollars, which is commonly referred to as the par value.

USING ALTMAN Z-SCORES

The creditworthiness of the issuer is the basis for assigning distinct credit ratings to bonds. Credit ratings are a component of a grading system that is conducted by agencies specializing in credit ratings. The aforementioned agencies assess the creditworthiness of both corporate and government bonds, as well as the capacity of the entity to reimburse these loans. Credit ratings provide valuable information to investors by delineating the level of risk associated with investment opportunities.

How do bond ratings relate to the 18.6-Year Real Estate Cycle? In 1967, NYU Stern Finance Professor Edward Altman created a powerful statistical formula that predicted the bankruptcy of public and private companies.

You see, the Altman Z-score is a magical concoction of profitability, leverage, liquidity, solvency, and activity ratios that, when mixed together just right, can help predict the financial health of a company. A score of zero on the Z-score scale means that the company is likely headed toward bankruptcy, while a score of three or higher indicates that the company is financially sound and secure.

Now, how does this relate to the real estate cycle, you might ask? Well, the Z-score has proven to be an excellent tool for predicting the ups and downs of the real estate market. Specifically, Altman found that there is a strong correlation between Z-score readings, and this can be applied to the 18.6 real estate cycle.

When the Z-score of a company in the real estate industry is high, it indicates that the company is financially stable and well-positioned for success. As a result, these companies are more likely to invest in new projects and developments, leading to a surge in real estate activity and growth. This growth phase of the cycle can last for fourteen years.

On the other hand, when the Z-score of real estate companies is low, it suggests that many companies in the industry are struggling to stay afloat and that the overall health of the market is declining. During this contraction phase of the cycle, real estate activity slows down, and prices can drop significantly.

This is where the Altman Z-scores truly shine, as they can help predict when companies are most at risk of going bankrupt and which are most likely to weather the storm.

Chapter Nine
The Domino Effect: Shanghai, London, and Sidney

Global house prices are now more synchronized than ever before in history.

Phillip J. Anderson, The Secret Life of Real Estate and Banking

The periphery of Beijing is characterized by extensive housing developments that bear a striking resemblance to one another. These projects, which are still under construction, cover vast areas of land that were previously occupied by villages and farmland on the outskirts of the city.

The global housing market is in shambles, a complex web of uncertainty and chaos that has left homeowners and investors alike in a state of disarray. The real estate bubble, which was once a beacon of hope and prosperity, has now been exposed for what it truly is: a ticking time bomb that threatens to detonate at any moment.

The 18.6-year housing cycle, the longest and most significant since the 2008 crisis, has ushered in a new era of instability and unpredictability, leaving even the most experienced industry experts scratching their heads in bewilderment.

The impact of this cycle can be felt all around the world, with cities such as Shanghai, London, and Sydney bearing the brunt of its destructive force. Unaffordability and soaring house prices have become hallmarks of the crisis, pricing individuals out of the market and leaving them with no hope of ever achieving the dream of homeownership.

This crisis is not just a problem for those directly involved in the housing market. It is a threat to the very foundations of our global economy. The ripple effects of this crisis can be felt across industries and borders, with the potential to cause irreparable damage to the world's financial infrastructure.

In the early 1990s, the lifting of restrictions on the purchase of private property marked a significant shift in the Chinese government's stance towards private property, which had been hostile under Maoist rule for several decades. As a result, a middle class emerged in mainland China, which displayed a keen interest in the fluctuation of house prices compared to their Western counterparts.

The Chinese Communist Party's credibility is at risk due to the deteriorating real estate market, which poses a threat to the middle class that currently serves as the government's primary support base.

Over a prolonged period, Beijing has endeavored to control prices. However, succumbed to stakeholder influence on multiple occasions. Presently, China is abandoning those endeavors completely with the aspiration of revitalizing the bubble that formerly served as the foundation for its economic expansion.

In contrast to the norm in many developing countries, the urban population in China was predominantly granted pre-existing rights to equity, resulting in a comparatively seamless shift from tenant status to land ownership.

In China, private ownership of land is not permitted; however, individuals have the option to lease land from the government for a duration of 70 years.

COLLAPSING CHINESE REAL ESTATE

The Chinese real estate market is in shambles, and the root cause can be traced back to the corruption and greed of developers. Incomplete building of apartments, defrauding Chinse homebuyers, and other corrupt practices have left a trail of destruction in their wake. The result is a market collapse, leaving homeowners and investors alike in a state of panic.

The situation has become so dire that Chinese citizens are taking matters into their own hands, protesting by holding mortgage parties.

These mortgage parties are a form of collective action where homeowners refuse to pay their mortgages in protest of the corrupt practices of developers. The aim is to send a message to the industry that enough is enough and that the Chinese people will not stand for being taken advantage of any longer.

The protests are a reflection of the deep-rooted frustration and anger felt by Chinese homebuyers, who have been left in a vulnerable position due to the corruption of developers. The incomplete building of apartments has left many families without a place to call home, and the defrauding of buyers has left many others in financial ruin.

Moreover, there are several other corrupt real estate practices that have been observed in China, including:

*Land Hoarding, where developers purchase large tracts of land and sit on them, waiting for the value to increase before building on them, which limits the amount of available land for development and drives up prices.

*Illegal construction in which developers often ignore safety regulations and building codes, leading to poorly constructed buildings that are at risk of collapse.

*False advertising, where developers advertise their properties with inflated square footage and exaggerated amenities that are not actually available, deceiving potential buyers.

*Insider trading, where some developers use their connections with government officials to gain access to valuable land and secure favorable policies, allows them to profit unfairly.

*Bribery, where developers bribe officials to gain access to land, permits, and other benefits, giving them an unfair advantage in the market.

*Shadow banking records are held apart from normal Chinese banking records, making them difficult to monitor and regulate. Shadow banking transactions and records are not included in official banking records maintained by the People's Bank of China.

*Shadow banks use WMPs, trust loans, and asset-backed securities that are not fully disclosed to investors.

*Shadow banking assets in China totaled approximately U.S. 7.5 trillion dollars in 2019, accounting for roughly 34% of the country's total banking assets.

Essentially, the decline in home values and homebuyers has also added to the financial burden of the company, resulting in unpaid suppliers and construction workers. The Chinese companies have issued numerous bonds, and are in distress worth only 25 cents on the dollar. This has led to solvency and liquidity problems for the company, which could have a contagion effect on other Asian Tiger countries, UK, Australia, and Third World countries.

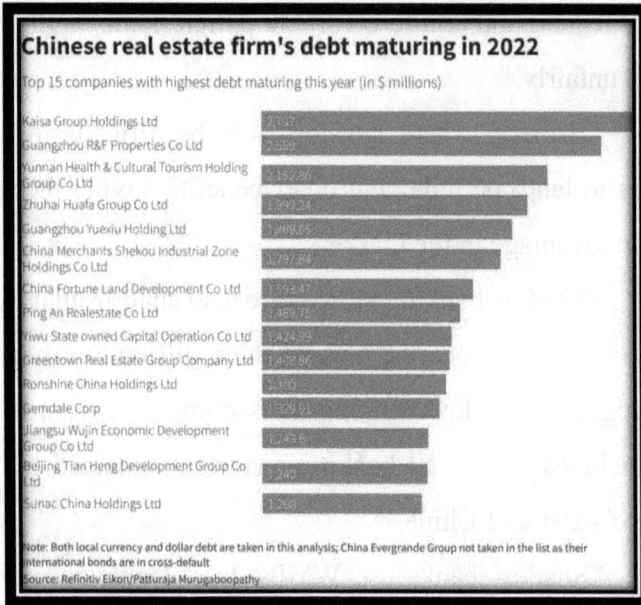

Chinese real estate firm's debt maturing in 2022

Top 15 companies with highest debt maturing this year (in $ millions)

Company	Debt ($ millions)
Kaisa Group Holdings Ltd	2,797
Guangzhou R&F Properties Co Ltd	2,659
Yunnan Health & Cultural Tourism Holding Group Co Ltd	2,152.06
Zhuhai Huafa Group Co Ltd	1,990.24
Guangzhou Yuexiu Holding Ltd	1,769.65
China Merchants Shekou Industrial Zone Holdings Co Ltd	1,797.84
China Fortune Land Development Co Ltd	1,593.47
Ping An Realestate Co Ltd	1,460.75
Yiwu State owned Capital Operation Co Ltd	1,424.99
Greentown Real Estate Group Company Ltd	1,409.86
Ronshine China Holdings Ltd	1,310
Gemdale Corp	1,278.91
Jiangsu Wujin Economic Development Group Co Ltd	1,243.6
Beijing Tian Heng Development Group Co Ltd	1,240
Sunac China Holdings Ltd	1,240

Note: Both local currency and dollar debt are taken in this analysis; China Evergrande Group not taken in the list as their international bonds are in cross-default
Source: Refinitiv Eikon/Patturaja Murugaboopathy

If the top five Chinese developers, Vanke, Greentown China Holding, Evergrande, Country Gardens, and Greenland Group, are shut out of the global bond market and cannot raise funds to solve their liquidity problems, it could have significant implications for China's economy and the global financial system.

The Chinese real estate giant Evergrande has been facing significant economic challenges due to its mounting debt and declining home values. The company has around 1,300 real estate properties in 280 Chinese cities, and its debt default on Chinese Dollar Denominated bonds has resulted in the locking out of Chinese developers from the global debt markets.

This is due to cross defaults with Chinese banks, making it difficult for Evergrande to obtain further financing to sustain its operations.

First, these companies are major players in China's real estate market, and their inability to access funding could result in a significant slowdown in the construction and development of new properties. This could lead to a decline in economic growth, potential job losses, and a decline in property prices.

Secondly, the default of these major developers could result in a loss of confidence in the broader Chinese financial system. Investors may begin to question the stability of other Chinese companies and the government's ability to manage the situation.

Thirdly, the impact could be felt beyond China's borders, with the potential for contagion effects on their emerging markets and developed economies that have financial ties with China. This could result in a wider market correction, a decline in investor sentiment, and a potential slowdown in global economic growth.

Developed economies such as the UK and Australia

could also be affected by the Chinese real estate crash. Both countries have significant trade links with China, and a slowdown in the Chinese economy could impact the demand for their exports.

Additionally, if Chinese investors who have invested heavily in the UK and Australian real estate markets begin to sell their properties, it could result in a significant drop in property prices in these countries.

What are the specific Chinese industries that will be impacted by the real estate crash:

*The real estate market is a major source of demand for construction activity in China. A housing collapse would likely lead to a significant decline in construction activity, which would impact home builders, building materials manufacturers, construction equipment suppliers, and the Chinese steel industry.

*A housing collapse would lead to a decline in housing prices, which would impact real estate agents, property management firms, and Chinese real estate investment trusts (REITs).

*A housing collapse could lead to significant losses for banks and other financial institutions that have exposure to the real estate markets. Chinese banks have the lowest capital in 30 years. Many Shanghai residents have experienced frozen ATM cards and Government lead ATM card suspension campaigns.

*A decline in the housing market could impact consumer confidence and impact department stores, supermarkets, and consumer electronics.

*The real estate market is a major driver of demand for building materials and appliances in China. A housing collapse would likely lead to a decline in demand for these products.

It is commonly believed that this lease can be renewed indefinitely. Retired urban baby boomers commonly acquired their property at a nominal cost from their work unit, also known as danwei.

Following the establishment of the market, there was a notable escalation in the prices of residential properties, which continued to rise steadily over time. Real estate has emerged as the most dependable investment option for Chinese households, prompting them to resort to all possible means to secure a position in the property market.

The Chinese populace has demonstrated a preference for investing in real estate, as the stock markets are perceived as unreliable and susceptible to government interference. In fact, approximately 70% of Chinese wealth is held in real estate. Additionally, it is worth noting that land sales continue to serve as the primary source of income for provincial administrators who have been accused of corruption.

Historically, prices have experienced fluctuations. However, the current situation is unprecedented for a multinational investment firm and developer. Ever Grande began to unravel in early 2022. This eventuality has been long-anticipated, yet Chinese President Xi Jinping appeared complacent and did not view it as a serious cause for concern. The situation has brought the bubble closer to bursting than ever before.

Despite the decline in sales and construction activity, housing prices have remained resiliently unaffected. This can be attributed to the substantial amount of venture capital invested in unsold properties and the strong opposition on mainland streets against any measures aimed at regulating prices.

Presently, Chinese authorities are endeavoring to stimulate the market instead of dampening it.

In early 2022, several municipal governments initiated a relaxation of restrictions in the hopes of mitigating declines in birth rates and home purchasing.

These efforts were implemented in a fragmented manner until national regulators intervened in November

2022, announcing a series of credit-easing measures aimed at providing reassurance to prospective homebuyers.

UK AND AUSTRALIAN CHINESE DOMINOS

The UK housing market has experienced a period of strain subsequent to the implementation of the "mini-budget" by the former Prime Minister, Liz Truss, in September. This decision led to a withdrawal of approximately 40% of all mortgage products from the UK market by lenders due to concerns regarding the escalation of interest rates.

The property sector in the United Kingdom has exhibited a lack of growth in recent months, which can be attributed to the Bank of England's persistent efforts to curb double-digit inflation through aggressive interest rate hikes. It was forecasted that the nation was embarking on its lengthiest economic downturn in history.

According to the Office for Budget Responsibility (OBR), an independent entity, there is a projected unprecedented decline in the living standards of households in the United Kingdom.

What are some of the economic dominos that will fall with a real estate collapse:

*A UK housing collapse would impact home builders, building materials, manufacturers, and construction equipment suppliers.

*The British real estate bubble would create havoc and collapse for real estate agents, property management firms, and (REITS).

*A UK housing collapse could lead to significant losses for banks with a mismatch of short and long-term maturities and a run of the bank. Moreover, financial services companies would become less profitable and lead to job losses in the sector.

*Many UK retailers would be heavily impacted by a loss of consumer confidence. The retail industry would have major revenue losses are department stores, supermarkets, and fashion retailers.

*The financial shock of the real estate collapse would result in a decline in the tourism industry. The reality is that people may be less likely to travel or spend money on leisure activities. The related industries of hotels, restaurants, and tour operators would suffer huge losses.

The Australian housing market is subject to intense scrutiny and debate due to its significant impact on the country's economy, with particular attention paid to the possibility of property bubbles and subsequent crashes. The prosperity of Australia's households and financial markets is largely reliant on property investments.

The recent fluctuation of Australia's property market is noteworthy for its rapidity and magnitude. The pandemic has resulted in a significant surge in housing prices, largely attributed to the historically low-interest rates that facilitated easier access to credit and attracted more buyers to the market.

Undoubtedly, a decline in housing prices has transpired subsequent to mid-2022, which coincided with the Reserve Bank of Australia's (RBA) initiation of raising the cash rate for the first time in more than ten years as a countermeasure to the escalation of inflation.

According to data from CoreLogic, a research firm specializing in the property industry, over 50% of the nation's suburban markets for houses and units experienced unprecedented declines in value from peak to trough in 2022. The research update of February 2023 indicated that a decline of 13% in national home values would be necessary to attain the levels observed in March 2020.

To clarify, the current rate of decline in value does not currently align with the level of value that was added during the period of 2020-2022. There exists a divergence of opinions regarding the potential deceleration or acceleration of the decline.

The Australian real estate collapse would be in the

dead center of the real estate cycle. The downfall of the following sectors would create panic:

*Australian construction would be impacted by home builders, building materials, manufacturers, and construction equipment suppliers. These companies may be highly leveraged and carry heavy debt loads.

*The real estate horror stories are circulating in the popular media and creating major problems for real estate agents, property management firms, and (REITS).

*The black swan events will be hitting the Australian banking system. Many banks and financial institutions that have exposure to the housing market are in great danger of bankruptcy. Many financial service companies will lose profitability status and suffer large job losses in this sector.

*Australian retail sector is greatly exposed to the collapse of consumer confidence, and new depression psychology will result in retail boycotts. The major department stores, supermarkets, and fashion retailers have high exposure to this recessionary psychology.

*The Australian tourism industry is predicated on the boom period of the real estate cycle. The problem is that people may be less likely to travel or spend money on leisure activities. This is a dire warning for hotels, restaurants, and tour operators.

*The Australian mining industry may face a domestic and international collapse of demand for their resources. Australia is closely tied to the housing market, as it supplies many of the raw materials used in construction. A housing collapse could lead to a decline in demand for these products, which could impact mining companies.

Adam Slater of Oxford Economics said that rapid increases in housing debt or leverage make sudden increases in home values more concerning. Since the 1970s, prices have increased quickly along with the share of mortgage credit in GDP, which has increased significantly (on average, from 20% to over 60%).

Some of the biggest housing booms, including those in the 1920s, 1980s, and 2000s, have also been preceded or accompanied by rapid credit growth.

WORLD HOUSING PRICES

Oxford Economics estimates suggest that house prices in advanced economies may be around 10% overvalued versus long-term trends, albeit with considerable variation between economies.

This boom, while not as pronounced as the one that preceded the global financial crisis, is still one of the biggest since 1900,

Currently, house prices look around 9% higher than long-term trend levels, as defined by data-smoothing filters to remove cyclical fluctuations. Looking at long-run price-to-rent ratios compared to trends suggests prices may be overvalued by about 11%.

By comparison, in the last boom that peaked in 2006, the estimated overvaluation was 13%-15%.

Since 1900, three broad phases have been visible in world house prices: a stable period to the 1960s, steady growth to the 1990s, and accelerated growth since then. Prices cycle around these trends, with the duration of cycles often long.

The current housing upturn is already quite lengthy at around a decade, with the weighted real price rise of 43% also high in historical comparison. The current boom looks to be perhaps the second-longest and third-largest (in terms of price rises) since 1900.

The boom in housing prices since the 1990s has been associated with the rapid expansion of mortgage credit. But in this upturn, although mortgage lending is showing signs of picking up, growth has not been very rapid compared to the period before the global financial crisis.

GLOBAL HOUSING SHORTAGE

Some evidence suggests the longer a housing boom

continues, the bigger the risk of a large reversal. Looking at individual economies, risk indicators show a varied picture: the riskiest markets look to be the Netherlands, Canada, Sweden, Germany, and France.

The upcoming year or two may present a favorable opportunity for prospective buyers to acquire properties from apprehensive investors or sellers with a strong incentive to sell.

During the upcoming market downturn, investors are likely to favor rental properties that generate positive cash flow and can be held for an extended period of time. These properties may also offer the potential for capital appreciation.

Given the current and anticipated rise in interest rates, it is plausible that financial outcomes may not be as favorable in 2023 compared to previous years.

Individuals who possess the capability to make cash purchases or utilize low Loan To Value financing have the opportunity to capitalize on favorable transactions. According to the World Bank, by 2025, approximately 1.6 billion individuals may be affected by the housing crisis.

The current housing crisis is being exacerbated by a number of factors, including but not limited to shortages in land, lending, labor, and materials.

According to UN-Habitat, there is a pressing need to construct 96,000 affordable dwellings on a daily basis to accommodate the projected 3 billion individuals who will require suitable housing by 2030.

According to data from the International Monetary Fund, the rate of growth in housing expenses has outpaced that of incomes in the majority of countries.

According to research conducted on 200 cities worldwide, it was discovered that 90% of them were deemed unaffordable for habitation, as the average cost of a home was more than three times the average income.

As per a study conducted by Moody's Analytics, there exists a deficit of 1.5 million homes in the United States.

According to the study titled "Overcoming the Nation's Daunting Housing Supply Shortage," the current housing supply for sale or rent in the country is at its lowest point in the past three decades.

According to a study conducted by Moody, the primary reasons for the housing shortage in the United States are attributed to the scarcity of land, lending opportunities, labor, and materials, which have been persisting since the financial crisis of 2008.

The escalation of expenses and reduction of profit

margins have been induced by this phenomenon experienced by builders. According to Moody's Analytics, the motivation to construct additional residences, particularly those with lower profit margins, such as affordable housing, is reduced.

The COVID-19 pandemic has been attributed to exacerbating the pre-existing housing crisis, as individuals seeking additional living space during periods of lockdown have contributed to increased demand for both purchasing and renting properties.

The current phenomenon has been fueled by historically low-interest rates in various countries, resulting in reduced borrowing costs.

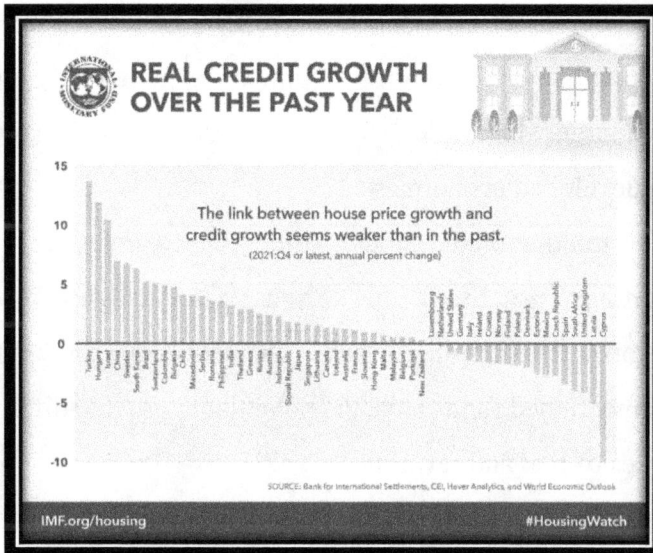

REAL CREDIT GROWTH OVER THE PAST YEAR

The link between house price growth and credit growth seems weaker than in the past.
(2021:Q4 or latest, annual percent change)

SOURCE: Bank for International Settlements, CEI, Haver Analytics, and World Economic Outlook

IMF.org/housing   #HousingWatch

RISE AND FALL OF INTERNATIONAL ETF

The critical question becomes whether or not to

invest in International ETFs. The International ETF market has become one of the fastest-growing areas for professional investors. The extra diversification gives a margin of safety to an investor's portfolio. What is an International ETF?

Any exchange-traded fund (ETF) that invests specifically in securities with a foreign base is considered an international ETF. The focus may be global, regional, or on a particular nation, and it may include fixed-income or equity securities.

International ETFs are typically passively invested in relation to an underlying benchmark index, but the index can differ significantly between different fund managers.

Some funds can offer excellent diversification by investing in a large number of companies, particularly those with a large worldwide reach or those that invest in nations with developed economies.

International funds offer U.S. investors the opportunity to invest in various asset classes across developed, emerging, and frontier markets. The aforementioned funds have the potential to provide different degrees of risk and reward.

International funds are managed across diverse asset classes, in addition to taking into account country-specific factors. The investment landscape offers a wide range of options, with debt and equity funds being the most prevalent among them.

American investors who aim to adopt a more cautious investment strategy have the option to allocate their funds toward government or corporate debt securities.

Equity funds provide diversified portfolios of stock investments that can be managed to achieve various objectives. Funds that allocate assets by combining debt and equity can offer a more equitable investment portfolio while also providing the chance to invest in specific global regions.

Adopting a global perspective towards investments can offer diversification and multiple avenues to capitalize on the expansion of the global economy, which is beneficial for both novice and experienced investors.

Investing in foreign markets may appear intricate; however, there exist exchange-traded funds (ETFs) that are designed to simplify the process and facilitate international investment for individuals in the United States.

The act of investing in foreign assets may seem superfluous to certain individuals; however, it can function as a beneficial safeguard against domestic market volatility and offers the possibility of increased returns in both established and developing markets.

Prior to engaging in international investment, it is

essential to comprehend the classification of global markets, as each nation and geographical area presents distinct risk and reward profiles.

The primary classifications are established, evolving, and nascent markets.

Developed markets are typically characterized by countries that possess well-established capital markets, comprehensive regulatory frameworks, sophisticated infrastructure, and other factors that contribute to economic stability.

This category includes nations such as the United Kingdom, Switzerland, and Japan. Consequently, their investment portfolios exhibit a high degree of similarity with those of the United States.

Emerging markets are characterized by rapid economic growth, which is frequently propelled by youthful demographics, infrastructure upgrades, technological innovations, and increased consumer expenditures. Brazil, India, and South Korea are among the countries that serve as illustrations.

The act of allocating resources to emerging markets offers prospects for greater yields compared to developed economies. Nonetheless, it is important to note that these nations are also more susceptible to economic and political volatility, which increases the likelihood of financial setbacks.

THE 2008 FALL OF INTERNATIONAL ETFS

In 2007, emerging markets were the belle of the ball, raising an impressive 39.38%. Investors were flocking to these regions, hoping to ride the wave of economic growth and development. But oh, how quickly fortunes can change! In 2008, emerging markets crashed and burned, posting a dismal -43.38% return. Ouch! That's a drop that could make even the toughest investor wince.

So, what happened? Well, as we all know, 2008 was the year of the global financial crisis. The real estate market in the United States, which had been booming for years, finally hit a wall and began to collapse.

The subprime mortgage crisis that had been building for years finally burst, causing a ripple effect throughout the financial system. Banks were failing left and right, and investors were panicking. In this environment, emerging markets were particularly vulnerable.

But here's the thing: 2009 was a different story entirely. Emerging markets bounced back with a vengeance, posting a staggering 78.51% return. How did they manage to do it?

Well, for one thing, the worst of the financial crisis

was over by then. The Federal Reserve backstopped the Transatlantic financial system. This means the Federal Reserve sent trillions to the European banking community. Governments around the world had stepped into stabilizing the financial system, and investors were feeling more confident.

Many emerging markets had strong fundamentals, with low debt and growing middle classes. And some countries, especially China, had implemented massive stimulus packages to keep the world economy from collapsing.

One of the great investment tools to look at the different investment rates of return is called Jay Kloepfter's "Periodic Table of Investment Returns." This chart will give you a yearly rate of return for emerging markets. This will help estimate the value of an International ETF and the coming real estate collapse.

It's not simple to plan for the long-term security of your wealth, especially if that future includes a period when the real estate crash creates a financial panic. But before you make any concrete choices concerning your wealth, it's essential to give some thought to your financial plan.

Chapter Ten
AI Real Estate 2.0

The greatest shortcoming of the human race is our inability to understand exponential growth.

-Albert Allen Bartlett

The use of AI is rapidly expanding across industries. Currently, it is used to power autonomous vehicles, locate prime spots for new stores, and screen for cancer. The real estate sector has also adapted to the new era. Real estate agents are beginning to incorporate AI into their work by using algorithms and data pipelines.

Artificial intelligence (AI) is transforming the real estate industry in unprecedented ways, revolutionizing the way investors and other stakeholders operate within the market.

The six major outcomes of AI in real estate—predictive analytics, risk assessment, cost optimization, real-time monitoring, data-driven decision-making, and scenario planning—are providing real estate investors with a competitive edge, giving them the ability to make informed decisions with greater speed and accuracy.

Predictive analytics is a powerful tool that enables real estate investors to gain insights into future market trends, property valuation, and other crucial factors affecting the industry.

By analyzing vast amounts of data, AI algorithms can identify patterns and make predictions that allow investors to make informed decisions. Predictive analytics helps investors anticipate future market movements and take advantage of opportunities before they arise.

Risk assessment is another critical outcome of AI in real estate. By analyzing past data, AI can identify patterns and potential risks associated with a particular property or location. Real estate investors can use this information to minimize their risks and make informed decisions that lead to successful investments.

Cost optimization is yet another vital outcome of AI in real estate. By analyzing past and present data, AI algorithms can identify cost-saving opportunities in property management and maintenance. These algorithms can suggest strategies that help investors reduce costs without compromising on the quality of the property.

Real-time monitoring is also a game-changing outcome of AI in real estate. With sensors and cameras installed in properties, AI algorithms can monitor and analyze data in real-time.

Investors can gain insights into property usage

patterns, maintenance needs, and tenant behavior, enabling them to make informed decisions quickly. Real-time monitoring enables investors to act promptly and efficiently, thereby improving their overall ROI

Data-driven decision-making is another significant outcome of AI in real estate. With AI-powered data analytics, real estate investors can make informed decisions based on objective data rather than subjective intuition.

AI algorithms can analyze vast amounts of data, identifying patterns and trends that human analysis may miss. This enables investors to make informed decisions that lead to profitable investments, giving them a competitive edge over their peers.

Lastly, scenario planning is a powerful outcome of AI in real estate. By simulating various scenarios and outcomes, AI algorithms can help investors plan for different eventualities, making informed decisions that lead to successful investments.

Scenario planning enables investors to test different strategies and evaluate their impact on their investment portfolio, enabling them to make better decisions that lead to long-term success.

In 2018, a real estate transaction powered by AI marked the first of several applications of AI in the sector.

Two Philadelphia homes for a total of 26 million dollars were acquired as a result of this deal. The "soon-to-market detection" AI technique was used to purchase the properties.

Finding new clients who are interested in their listings is a challenge for real estate salespeople. They waste a lot of time talking to people who aren't going to become customers. Using information gathered from websites, landing pages, and digital advertising, artificial intelligence is able to pinpoint the most promising leads.

THE NEW AI REAL ESTATE COMPANIES

If you're looking for a needle in a haystack, Data Flik might just be the magnet you need. This innovative AI company specializes in predictive modeling for identifying motivated sellers, using skip tracing to pinpoint them with the utmost accuracy and doing so at the lowest possible costs.

With a 67% prediction rate, Data Flik is quickly becoming the go-to resource for anyone in the real estate industry looking to get ahead.

One shining example of Data Flik's success is its work in Maricopa County, Arizona. Using their cutting-edge technology and data analysis, Data Flik identified 119 neighborhoods in the area and found the top 25 that sold a whopping 70% of all properties in the county. This information is gold for real estate agents, wholesalers, house flippers, and real estate investors alike.

Imagine having this kind of insider knowledge at your fingertips. With Data Flik, it's no longer a pipe dream. By utilizing their predictive modeling and skip-tracing capabilities, you can find motivated sellers faster and more efficiently than ever before. This gives you a competitive edge in the real estate market and can help you close deals faster with greater confidence.

E-commerce enterprises are currently experiencing advantages from the utilization of artificial intelligence-driven consumer applications and chatbots. Real estate enterprises are also making progress in this regard by utilizing identical technology to furnish tailored content directly to potential clients.

The impact of chatbots on content marketing is readily apparent, as it has significant implications for the future of the real estate industry.

Real Estate Trainer recommends that agents promptly respond to inquiries from prospective clients within a five-minute timeframe.

According to the source, a significant majority of potential leads, specifically over 78%, tend to remain loyal to the real estate agent who responds to their inquiry first.

Artificial intelligence (AI) enabled chatbots have the ability to address common customer inquiries without utilizing aggressive marketing tactics or desperate attempts to obtain a potential customer's personal information.

Artificial Intelligence (AI) can enable real estate firms to determine optimal periods for property acquisition or sale and predict forthcoming sale or rental rates.

The utilization of a regression algorithm that takes into account various property features such as size, age, number of rooms, and home décor can be employed to determine a feasible price range.

Through the integration of the market, it becomes possible to track and analyze all user-generated activity data, thereby yielding valuable insights.

The utilization of Artificial Intelligence extends to the domain of real estate management, facilitating more intelligent and efficient operations.

In the context of expansive real estate, such as office complexes and corporate edifices, a significant portion of the budget may be consumed by the phenomenon of underutilization.

Inadequate management of commercial space frequently results in employee discontentment. Artificial Intelligence (AI) can aid professionals in real estate management to optimize office space utilization through the use of sensors and Internet of Things (IoT) devices.

By utilizing wireless networking technology and Internet of Things (IoT) devices, it is possible to analyze data and extract valuable insights. The aforementioned insights have the potential to assist managers in enhancing their decision-making abilities with regard to office spaces.

Natural language recognition tools enable individuals to communicate with physical environments, and through the use of artificial intelligence, the comprehension of user requirements can be significantly enhanced.

The process of seeking a new residence can be challenging due to the multitude of variables that must be evaluated prior to making a purchase. Conventional search engines offer limited filtering options and frequently present the purchaser with an abundance of search results to sift through.

AI-based algorithms are utilized in this context. AI-driven personalization tools can detect the user's inclinations and provide recommendations accordingly.

Certain applications have the capability to analyze user-generated photographs and extract pertinent data, including but not limited to favored flooring types, color schemes, and building materials.

The system has the capability to compare the preferences of the buyer with those of other individuals who share similar interests and generate a distinctive portfolio for the buyer. Anticipating forthcoming events is arguably the most salient characteristic of Artificial Intelligence.

The real estate sector is a high-stakes industry that offers significant rewards, and the capacity to anticipate results is exceedingly valuable.

Artificial intelligence (AI) systems have the capability to analyze historical data and market trends in order to generate precise forecasts regarding future market trends.

The implementation of artificial intelligence has proven to be a highly effective tool in the realm of real estate investment.

Conventional real estate agents are familiar with the customary approach of assessing a property based on its covered area dimensions, quality of the renovation, and other typical characteristics.

Rest. AI is a cutting-edge real estate company that utilizes innovative AI technology to revolutionize the way property listings are created, managed, and marketed. Through advanced image recognition and data enrichment solutions, Restb.AI is able to transform the traditional real estate landscape and provide unparalleled services to clients.

One of the primary areas where Restb.AI's technology shines is in property descriptions. Using a combination of image recognition and data enrichment tools,

Restb.AI is able to analyze a property's visual features and translate them into engaging descriptive language. This means that potential buyers can quickly and easily understand the unique characteristics of a property, even if they have never seen it in person, from the stunning views to the sleek modern architecture, Restb. AI's property descriptions leave nothing to the imagination.

In addition to property descriptions, Restb. AI also excels in real estate image tagging. By utilizing cutting-edge image recognition technology, Restb AI is able to accurately label every aspect of a property's visual features.

This includes everything from the type of flooring to the style of the kitchen cabinets. With this level of detail, buyers can quickly filter through properties to find the ones that best meet their needs and preferences.

Restb.AI's image recognition technology is also utilized in visual property conditions by analyzing images of a property's interior and exterior, Restb. AI is able to identify any potential issues or concerns, such as water damage or foundation problems. This allows buyers to make informed decisions about which properties to consider and which ones to avoid.

Another area where Restb.AI's technology shines is in visual similarities for future home choices. By analyzing the visual features of a property, Restb.AI can provide recommendations for similar properties that a potential buyer may be interested in.

This allows buyers to quickly and easily find properties that meet their specific needs and preferences.

Finally, Restb.AI's technology includes duplicate listing detections. By analyzing property images and data, Restb.AI can identify duplicate listings and ensure that each property is represented accurately and fairly. This eliminates confusion for buyers and ensures that sellers are not misrepresented or taken advantage of.

In the realm of luxury real estate, the establishment of an appropriate pricing strategy is frequently a determining factor in the achievement of a successful transaction.

Lead generation is a common issue that arises in the real estate industry. Artificial Intelligence (AI) has the potential to distinguish between prospective property buyers and individuals who are merely browsing for informational purposes.

Finally, it is worth noting that a significant aspect of

the real estate sector pertains to mortgage lending, which is inherently reliant on data analysis.

When it comes to the mortgage industry, providing exceptional customer service is the key to building lasting relationships with clients.

By using artificial intelligence (AI) and machine learning to better understand the emotional needs and desires of borrowers, mortgage companies can create a more personalized and engaging experience that sets them apart from the competition.

One company that's leading the way in this regard is Southwest Mortgage Company, which has recently introduced a new AI-powered virtual assistant called AI Morgan.

Using cutting-edge technology and advanced algorithms, AI Morgan is able to interact with borrowers in a natural and conversational way, providing instant answers to common questions and guiding them through the mortgage application process with ease.

But what sets AI Morgan apart is its emphasis on empathetic technology by analyzing subtle cues in a borrower's voice and language.

AI Morgan is able to pick up on their emotional state and respond with empathy and understanding. This creates a more human-like interaction that can help to build trust and establish a positive rapport between the borrower and the mortgage company.

For example, if a borrower expresses frustration or confusion about a particular aspect of the mortgage process., AI Morgan can respond with language that acknowledges and addresses those emotions, such as "I understand how you feel, and I'm here to help you navigate this process as smoothly as possible."

Overall, the combination of emphatic technology and AI Morgan is a game-changer for mortgage companies like Southwest Mortgage Company.

By leveraging advanced AI machine learning to create a more personalized and emotionally intelligent experience intelligent for borrowers, companies can improve customer satisfaction, build stronger relationships and ultimately drive business success.

In order to be considered for a loan, various documents such as bank statements, credit histories, and proof of income are typically required. Financial institutions employ optical character recognition (OCR) technology to interpret written materials.

However, the limitation of OCR systems is their inability to identify unformatted documents. Artificial intelligence (AI) has the potential to enhance the analysis of information for lending decisions.

A new AI-powered feature from Zillow allows users to search for homes in a manner similar to that of conversing with friends and relatives.

Instead of starting with a location and having to filter their way to the properties they desire, home buyers may now immediately enter keywords into the Zillow search bar, such as "700,000 dollars homes in Charlotte with a backyard" or "open house near me with four bedrooms." Additionally, they have the option to save their searches and have Zillow notify them when new listings that qualify appear online.

The natural language search function on Zillow parses user queries and searches through millions of listing details to uncover the most pertinent results. The feature is also teaching machine learning models how to reply more effectively to search queries that contain natural, human-sounding language.

The first significant residential real estate marketplace to use this cutting-edge, AI-powered search engine is Zillow.

Zillow's most influential features, such as the Neural Zestimate® valuation, the best-personalized property suggestions, and the ability to create floor plans from panoramic pictures, are all made possible by AI and machine learning.

As part of its mission to provide the "housing super app" — a unified digital ecosystem of connected solutions for all the chores and services related to moving — the company continues to invest in technological innovation like AI.

When it comes to reaching high-income individuals in the real estate market, two names stand out from the rest: Wealth Engine 9 and Wealth X. These powerful screening tools have revolutionized the way real estate professionals connect with the ultra-affluent, providing invaluable insights and data-driven strategies for success.

Wealth Engine 9 is a cutting-edge platform that allows users to identify and target individuals based on a wide range of criteria, including wealth, assets, and lifestyle factors. With its sophisticated algorithms and advanced analytics,

Wealth Engine 9 provides real estate marketers with an unparalleled level of precision and accuracy, allowing them to tailor their messages and campaigns to the unique needs and preferences of each high-net-worth individual.

But where Wealth Engine 9 really shines is in its

ability to integrate seamlessly with other marketing tools and platforms, creating a comprehensive ecosystem of data-driven marketing strategies.

From email campaigns to social media advertising. Wealth Engine 9 empowers real estate professionals to engage with high-income clients on every level maximizing their reach and impact.

Meanwhile, Wealth-X is a game-changing resource for real estate marketers looking to connect with the world's wealthiest individuals. With its comprehensive database of over 300,000 ultra-high-net-worth individuals, Wealth-X provides unparalleled insights into the lifestyles, preferences, and investment habits of the global elite.

Through its powerful real and analysis, Wealth-X enables real estate professionals to better understand the needs and desires of high-net-worth individuals, allowing them to craft targeted marketing messages that resonate on a personal level.

With Wealth-X, real estate marketers can gain a competitive edge in the ultra-competitive world of high-end real estate.

When it comes to predicting the future, AI has a lot of advantages over human beings, and it's not hard to see why. One of the key advantages of AI over traditional

Superforecasting models is the sheer amount of data that it can analyze.

While human beings are limited by their cognitive capacities, AI has no such limitations. It can comb through massive data sets, identifying patterns and trends that would be impossible for a human being to spot.

With this level of insight, AI can provide more accurate and reliable predictions, giving individuals a competitive edge when it comes to anticipating future events.

Another advantage of AI is its ability to simulate different scenarios and predict the potential outcome of each scenario. The use of the AI program AlphaGo created a worldwide awareness of how AI won 4 out of 5 Go matches.

By running complex simulations, AI can provide individuals with a range of possible futures, enabling them to make more informed and data-driven decisions.

This is particularly useful in situations where there are multiple variables at play, such as in financial markets or complex geopolitical environments.

Perhaps one of the most exciting aspects of AI is its ability to learn and adapt over time. By continuously processing new data and analyzing its own performance, AI can improve its forecast and prediction accuracy, providing individuals with even more valuable insights.

As AI becomes more advanced, we can expect it to play an increasingly important role in shaping the way we think about the future and plan for the unknown.

In summary, AI has several advantages over human forecasting and prediction, including its ability to process vast amounts of data, simulate different scenarios, learn from past performance, and operate at scale.

The 21st century is an era of innovation and rapid technological advancement, and the world of real estate is not immune to these changes.

RISE OF AI SUPER FORECASTING

Over the course of this century, the real estate market will experience five major cycles, each lasting approximately 18.6 years. These cycles will shape the landscape of the industry, influencing trends in investment, construction, and development.

The first cycle, spanning from 2008-2026, was marked by a period of recovery following the global financial crisis of 2008. Neil Howe's The Fourth Turning creates a generational marker for this period.

The market saw a surge in demand for affordable housing, leading to a boom in the rental market. This cycle was characterized by an emphasis on sustainability and energy efficiency as the industry grappled with the impact of climate change and sought to reduce its carbon footprint. The real estate cycle will collapse in 2008 and 2026.

The second cycle, from 2026 to 2044, will see the widespread adoption of AI and machine learning in the real estate industry. With the rise of intelligent automation, banks and lenders will be able to analyze market trends and make predictions with greater accuracy than ever before. This will lead to more efficient decision-making and greater investments in areas with high growth potential. The real estate cycle will collapse in 2026 and 2044.

In the third cycle, spanning from 2044 to 2062 advances in robotics and automation will lead to the creation of smart cities.

These urban centers will be designed to be self-sustaining, with cutting-edge technology managing everything from transportation to energy consumption.

Cathie Woods Ark Investments will take place in this time period. The real estate market will adapt to this new reality, with developers focusing on constructing sustainable buildings that integrate seamlessly with the city's infrastructure. The real estate cycle will collapse in 2044 and 2062.

The fourth cycle, from 2062 to 2080, will see the

emergence of space-based real estate. With the increasing commercialization of space travel, the demand for extraterrestrial property will skyrocket.

Investors will seek to capitalize on this new market, investing in the development of habitats and research facilities on the moon and other celestial bodies. The real estate cycle will collapse in 2062 and 2080.

The final cycle, from 2080 to 2098, will be marked by the integration of AL and blockchain technology in the real estate market.

Smart contracts will revolutionize the way properties are bought and sold, with transactions taking place on decentralized, transparent platforms. This will lead to greater efficiency and reduced costs, making real estate more accessible to a wider range of individuals. The real estate cycle will collapse in 2080 and 2098.

AI EVOLUTION OF THE REAL ESTATE CYCLE

AI Superforecasting tools will revolutionize how real estate agents will do business in the future. Real estate agents who ignore the potential of AI Superforecasting tools may risk falling behind their competitors who are leveraging these technologies.

In today's data-driven world, real estate agents who can leverage the power of AI and machine learning to provide more accurate predictions and better serve their clients are likely to be more successful in the industry. The AI real estate market is expanding, whereas the traditional market is in a state of collapse.

What are some of the main reasons that real estate agents would use AI real estate Superforecasting:

*Increased accuracy: AI Superforecasting tools can provide more accurate predictions of market trends and property values, allowing agents to make better decisions and provide better service to their clients.

*Competitive advantage: Agents who can leverage AI Superforecasting tools to gain insights and stay ahead of the market are likely to have a competitive advantage over those who do not.

*Better risk management: AI Superforecasting tools can help agents identify potential risks and market downturns, allowing them to make more informed decisions and mitigate risk.

*Time savings: By automating the process of data analysis and prediction, AI Superforecasting tools can save real estate agents valuable time that can be used to focus on other important aspects of their business.

*Customized insights: AI Superforecasting tools can be customized to provide insights specific to a local market or particular property, helping agents make more informed decisions and better serve their clients.

In short, real estate agents who ignore the potential AI Superforecasting tools may be at a disadvantage in today's data-driven real estate industry, save time, and make more informed decisions that lead to greater success in the industry.

Dr. Herrera has developed the Nexus AI Superforecasting Model, which is designed to analyze the interrelationship among the 18.6- year Real Estate Cycle, Credit Cycle, and Distressed Credit Cycle. The model uses Artificial Intelligence techniques to identify and analyze the patterns and trends in these cycles and to provide insights into the potential impact of these cycles on the economy,

One of the major features of the Nexus AI Superforecasting Model is its ability to analyze large volumes of data from multiple sources, including financial markets, real estate markets, economic indicators, and other relevant sources.

The model uses machine learning algorithms to identify patterns and trends in this data and to make predictions about future economic conditions based on these patterns.

Another key feature of the Nexus AI

Superforecasting Model is its ability to identify the interrelationships among different economic cycles, including the 18.6 Real Estate Cycle, Credit Cycle, and Distressed Credit Cycle.

By analyzing these cycles together, the Superforecasting model can provide insights into how changes in one cycle may affect the others and how these changes may impact the broader economy.

One of the main outcomes of the Nexus AI Superforecasting Model is its ability to predict changes in economic conditions, such as shifts in real estate prices, changes in credit availability, and increases in distressed credit.

By providing early warnings of potential economic shifts, the model can help investors, policymakers, and other stakeholders make informed decisions about how to respond to these changes.

Overall, Dr. Herrera's Nexus AI Superforecasting Model represents an important contribution to the field of economic analysis, providing a powerful tool for understanding the interrelationships among different economic cycles and predicting changes in economic conditions.

In conclusion, the AI revolution will impact the real

estate industry is significant and far-reaching. Its predictive analytics and intelligent management solutions can help real estate professionals navigate the 18.6-year cycle and make more informed decisions about buying, selling, and investing in properties. With AI, real estate professionals have the power to shape the future of the industry and maximize their returns.

SELECTED BIBLIOGRAPHY

Anderson, Phillip J. The Secret Life of Real Estate and Banking . Texere Publishing Ltd. 2008

Calomris, Charles W. and Joseph R. Mason. Contagion and Bank Failures During the Great Depression. Federal Reserve Bank of Atlanta, 2003.

Eichholtz, Piet. Herengracht Index: 1628-1973. Real Estate Finance and Investment, 1997.

Fels, Rendigs. American Business Cycles, 1865-1867. Arno Press, 1978.

Foldvary, Fred. The Business Cycle. Edward Elgar Publishing, 1998.

Goldstain, Joshua S. Long Cycles. Yale University Press, 1998.

Gordon, John Steele. The Great Game: The emergence of Wall Street as a World Power, 1653-2000. Scribner, 1999.

Grant, James. The kTrouble with Prosperity: A Contrarian's Tale of Boom, Bust and Speculation. Crown Business, 1996.

Harrison, Fred. The Power of the Land. University of Texas Press, 1994.

Hogan, Chris. Everyday Millionaires. Ramsey Press, 2019.

Howe, Neil. The Fourth Turning is Here: What the Seasons of History Tell Us About How and When This Crisis Will End. Simon and Schuster, 2023.

Hoyt, Homer. One Hundred Years of Land Value. University of Nebraska Press, 1991.

Kai, Fu Lee and Chen Qiufan. AI 2041: Ten Visions of Our Future. Crown Publishing Group, 2021.

Kaku, Michio. Quantum Supremacy: How the Quantum Computer Will Change Everything. Doubleday, 2023.

Knowlton, Christopher. Bubble in the Sun. Simon & Schuster, 2020.

Leonard, Christopher. The Lords of Easy Money. Penguin Press, 2019.

Lewis, Michael. The Big Short. W.W. Norton & Company 2010.

 Marks, Howard Mastering the Market Cycle. Houghton Miflin Harcourt, 2019.

Menschell, Robert. Markets, Mobs and Mayhem: A Modern Look at the Madness of Crowds. Wiley, 2002.

Rothbard, Murray N. A History of Money and Banking in the United States: The Colonial Era to World War II. Ludwig von Mises Institute, 2002.

Rubino, John. Main Street, Not Wall Street. Wilely 2020.

Sobel, Robert. Panic on Wall Street: A History of America's Financial Disasters. Beard Books, 1999.

Tetlock, P.E. & Gardner, D. Superforecasting: The Art And Science of Prediction. Crown, 2015.

Tooze, Adam. Crashed: How a Decade of Financial Crises Changed the World. Penguin, 2018.

Tooze, Adam, Statistics and the German State: The Making of Modern Economic Knowledge, Cambridge University Press, 2001.

Werner, Richard. Princes of the Yen: Japan's Central Bankers and the Transformation of the Economy. Routledge, 2003.

ARTICLES

Diamond, Dougles, and Dybrig, "Bank Runs, Deposit Insurance, and Liquidity," Journal of Political Economy, 1983. https://www.legit.ng/business-economy/industry/1515730-roy-carroll-meet-college-dropout-owns-a-multi-billion-dollar-real-estate-empire/ ,

V. E. (2023, January 23). *Legit*. Retrieved from legit.ng: https://www.legit.ng/business-economy/industry/1515730-roy-carroll-meets-college-dropout-owns-a-multi-billion-dollar-real-estate-empire/

Kyle Mittan, U.C. (2020, August 11). *The University of Arizona* Retrieved from news.arizona.edu: https://news.arizona.edu/story/study-predicts-millions-unsellable-homes-could-upend-market

Lowrey, A. (2023, January 20). *How ChatGPT Will Destabilize White-Collar Work* Retrieved from msn.com: https://www.msn.com/en-us/news/technology/how-chatgpt-will-destabilize-white-collar-work/ar-AA16yBZM

Olick, D. (2022, November 1). *Homebuilders say they're on the edge of a steeper downturn as buyers pull back.* Retrieved from cnbc.com: https://www.cnbc.com/2022/10/31/homebuilders-say-steeper-downturn-is-coming-as-buyers-pull-back.html

Olick, D. (2022, September 20). *More homebuilders lower prices as sentiment falls for the ninth straight month.* Retrieved from cnbc.com: https://www.cnbc.com/2022/09/19/more-homebuilders-lower-prices-sentiment-falls-for-ninth-straight-month.html

Pettypiece, S. (2022, September 24). *The pandemic's real estate jobs boom is turning into a bust as layoffs hit.* Retrieved from nbcnews.com: https://www.nbcnews.com/politics/pandemics-real-estate-jobs-boom-turning-bust-layoffs-hit-rcna48811

Richardson, B. (2022, November 28). *Forbes.* Retrieved from Forbes.com: https://www.forbes.com/sites/brendarichardson/2022/11/28/home-prices-plunge-in-pandemic-boomtowns-as-the-market-slumps/?sh=14afc9003f6c

Santarelli, M. (2023, March 7). *Norada Real Estate Investments* Retrieved from Norada Real Estate: https://www.noradarealestate.com/blog/housing-prices/

Simpson, Herbert D. "Real Estate Speculation and the Depression". Journal of Political Economy, vol. 44, no. 2, 1936, pp. 147–158

TEAM, T. I. (2022, April 30). *Rent Control.* Retrieved from Investopedia.com: https://www.investopedia.com/terms/r/rent-control.asp

YouTube Connections

Sachs Realty: Sachs Realty YouTue, Nov. 10, 2019.

https://www.youtube.com/channel/UC7V8dJsmuFJ5QdHju
vW1g.

Real Estate Mindset: Real Estate Mindset. Youtube
uploaded by Real Mindset, 4 Mar. 2020.
https://youtube.com/channel/UC96slcoyRdRb8Jyp18Dw5B
w.

Revenuture Consulting: Reventure Consulting. YouTube,
uploaded by Reventure Consulting, 28 Jul. 2020,

https://www.youtube.com/Channel/UCvT3Mn
ZqfzftS9nS2qxU6IQ.

Scott Walters Report: Scott Walters Report. YouTube,
uploaded by Scott Walters Report, 12 Jan. 2021.

https://www.youtube
.com/channel/UCNkOxzCYOQMA2ZvOrmx-IBw.

Michael Bordenaro: Michael Bordenaro. YouTube,
uploaded by Michael Borenaro, 17 Dec. 2018

https://www.youtube.com/Channel/UCaVHhLJvEg
M17z15TNQeu5Q.

Orlando Miner: Orlando Mier: Orlando Miner. You Tube,
uploaded by Orlando Miner 3. Jul2018.

https:// www.youtube.com/ Orlando Channel

INDEX

Thank You!

www.ingramcontent.com/pod-product-compliance
Lightning Source LLC
Chambersburg PA
CBHW071214210326
41597CB00016B/1815